THE
WORKING
STIFF
COOKBOOK

Library of Congress Cataloging-in-Publication Data:
Sloan, Bob.
The working stiff cookbook: great food,
easy recipes/by Bob Sloan;
illustrations by Michael Klein.
p. cm.
Includes index.
ISBN 0-8118-1885-3
1. Quick and easy cookery. 2. Dinners and dining.
I. Title.
TX833.5.S63 1998
641.5'12—dc21   97-30798
CIP

Printed in Singapore

Designed by carole goodman

Distributed in Canada by Raincoast Books
8680 Cambie Street
Vancouver, B.C. V6P 6M9

10 9 8 7 6 5 4 3 2

Chronicle Books
85 Second Street
San Francisco, CA 94105

www.chroniclebooks.com

THE WORKING STIFF COOKBOOK

reat food! easy recipes!

by **bob** sloan

illustrations by **michael** klein

CHRONICLE BOOKS
SAN FRANCISCO

CONTENTS

Jumbo Shrimp; Swift Swordfish; 10-Minute Salmon; Fast
Flounder Thai Style; Sole in Foil; Chicken Breasts with
Artichokes and Mushrooms; Stir-Fry Furioso; Rosemary
Chicken Breast; Quick Chicken; Chicken Fajitas;
Southwestern-Style Oven-Fried Chicken; Fillet of Beef
with Wild Mushrooms; Burger Bliss; Jerk Skirt; Singular
Meat Loaves; Pork Chops with Orange Glaze; Pancakes;
Broiled Lamb Chops; Veal Piccata

one-pot dinners 65

Pan-Roasted Salmon; Cajun Monkfish; Providence Fish
Stew; Paella Rapido; Chicken Parmesan; Deluxe Chicken
Breast; Chicken Curry in a Hurry; Fast Turkey Chili;
Chicken with Porcini Mushrooms; Steak in a Brown
Paper Bag; Stuffed Flank Steak; Fritatta Rustica; Sicilian
Vegetable Stew; Vegetarian Skillet Chilaquiles

pasta 93

Spaghetti with Portobellos, Prosciutto, and Cream;
Linguini with Meat Sauce and Fennel; Lazy Man's
Lasagna; Fettucini with Smoked Salmon; Penne from
the Cupboard; Speedy Tortellini; Baked Penne; Thai
Vegetable Noodles

soups, salads & sandwiches 113

Grandma Sally's Easy Broccoli Soup; Sausage,
Escarole, and White Bean Soup; Butternut Squash
Soup; Portobello and Onion Sandwich; Potato Salad;
Egg Salad Sandwich; B.A.L.T.; Chicken and Smoked
Mozzarella Salad; Grilled Cheese Sandwich; Citrus
Shrimp Salad; Leftover Lo Mein; Leftover Wild Rice
Salad; Leftover Green Bean Salad; Eggs for Dinner;
Greek Salad in Pita Sandwich

INTRODUCTION

"hi, honey, i'm home!"

THE MANTRA OF THE FIFTIES, when all the men worked and all the women knew how to cook. These days it seems everybody works and no one knows how to cook. Instead of being the reward at the end of a long day's work, dinner has become a burden, a tiresome chore to be disposed of as expediently as possible.

But no matter how hard you work or how tired you are, you still have to eat. And if you have kids, well, they need to eat, too. The challenge for the Working Stiff is to cook something using his or her last gasp of energy. It's not always easy.

Here are the challenges most Working Stiffs face when it comes to making dinner:

shopping=going to stores
not buying the right stuff
getting too much
getting too little
getting lost in the aisles
waiting on endless lines
cooking=following a recipe
not having the time to shop
finding the energy
getting in over your head
not knowing the techniques
forgetting a key ingredient
needing fancy equipment
cooking something too long
cooking something too little
no one recognizes the food

The result of this reasoning is that the Working Stiff's cooking skills atrophy, and he or she becomes more reluctant to make dinner. Take-out, or what is euphemistically called Home Meal Replacement, becomes the preferred option. Or, putting a frozen pizza in the oven. Or, if you have kids, giving them ten bucks and letting them fend for themselves.

But even Working Stiffs know in their heart of hearts that families should gather around the dinner table, to eat and laugh and argue. And what brings them together best is the home-cooked meal. Now maybe it's not *every* night, and maybe these dinners aren't as elaborate as when Mom was in the kitchen all day, and maybe *everything* isn't made from scratch, but it's still home-cookin', the smell filling the house and nourishing everyone's body and soul.

This cookbook will give you the strategies, recipes, and, I hope, confidence to get a meal on the table. It assumes you have little excess time or energy and that you possess only a few basic cooking skills which you haven't spent a lot of effort cultivating. It also assumes that you want food that tastes good, is prepared using mostly fresh ingredients, and is low in fat. Cooking like it should be—easy recipes that are simple, flavorful, and fun.

Also included are tips to help you make preparations to fit around your schedule. Working Stiffs are encouraged to devote a few minutes each night to slicing and chopping to help ensure that the following evening's dinner goes together in a snap. And many of the dishes will provide you with leftovers that can be effortlessly transformed into a tasty lunch.

The book focuses on the main course, but it also includes a smattering of easy potato and grain dishes to serve on the side. As a Working Stiff myself, I realize you're probably pushing yourself to the max just getting the entrée together. To start thinking about side dishes might send you into the *"danger Will Robinson!"* mode. Making a side dish may be pushing the culinary envelope, leaving you wondering how they are ever going to be finished at the same time. No problem.

Just rely on the planning tips I've outlined in the recipes. And keep in mind that, once cooked, rice can stay covered in the pot off the heat for at least a half hour. Potatoes can easily be reheated. This gives plenty of margin for error in timing. Take advantage of it. Vegetables should be steamed, and since this only takes a few minutes, you can get them ready in the steamer and cook them just before you're about to serve the meal.

And then there's dessert. After working all day, there's a good chance you'll want dessert, though you may not want to make it. Some ripe fruit and a small bowl of ice cream or sorbet is usually more than satisfactory after dinner. But for those occasions when you're feeling inspired, or when you're bring- ing dessert to another Working Stiff's dinner party, I've included a few choice quick and easy recipes.

This may not be the cookbook you curl up with at night. I don't describe the aromas emanating from rustic soup pots simmering on Tuscan farmhouse stoves. I don't tantalize you with stories of meals I've had in Venetian trattorias, the owner joining me at my table to share century-old culinary secrets and then escorting me back to my hotel singing Rossini arias in the mist and moonlight. Instead, I

present easy recipes that make allowances for a
hectic schedule and will result in satisfying
and great-tasting meals for you, your family,
and your friends.

The Working Stiff Cookbook is not for
people who enjoy lousy food, who run from
flavor, who revel in blandness. It is for the
courageous, those cavalier individuals who may
not have the strongest cooking chops but are
willing to try because they know they deserve
a meal, at the end of a long day, that is satisfying to both their palate and their soul.

THE BASIC BASICS

THERE ARE THE BASICS, and then there are the *basic* basics.

the pantry

A well-stocked pantry is the next best thing to having Barbara Eden pop out of her genie bottle to cook dinner for you. Your pantry should have the following items:

anchovies
anchovy paste
artichoke hearts
asian sesame oil
baking powder
baking soda
balsamic vinegar
barbecue sauce
bread crumbs (unseasoned)
brown rice
canned beef stock
canned chicken stock
canned crushed tomatoes
canned whole tomatoes
cocoa
couscous
dried mushrooms
hot sauce
olive oil
pasta in various sizes and shapes
Pickapeppa sauce
roasted red bell peppers
salsa

soy sauce
sun-dried tomatoes packed in oil
teriyaki sauce
Thai fish sauce
tuna fish
vegetable oil
vegetable oil cooking spray
white wine vinegar
white rice
wild rice

essential pots & pans

two 10-inch skillets (the pan you'll
use most often, so it behooves you to
own two; a stainless steel skillet with
sloped sides and a cast iron skillet
with steeper sides)
4-quart soup pot with lid (a heavy
bottom helps prevent scorching)
8-quart pot with lid (for pasta)
two 2^1/$_2$-quart saucepans with lids
(for vegetables, mashed potatoes, rice)

9-by-13-inch Pyrex casserole

8-by-8-inch Pyrex casserole

11-by-17-inch stainless steel
   baking pan

pie pan

Bundt pan (for classy desserts that
   look like you spent a lot more time
   on them than you actually did)

how to tell a good pan
from a lousy one

The weight's a giveaway. A good pan is
heavy. It has substance. And that substance
usually is stainless steel or aluminum or some
combination of the two. All-Clad pots and pans
are the brand of choice for many chefs. Their
stainless-steel interior is an excellent cooking
surface, and the hidden copper layer evenly
and quickly distributes the heat. Cuisinart and
Calphalon are also good cookware lines. The
staff at a reputable kitchen store can help you
choose the pans you need. Keep in mind that

quality pots and pans last a lifetime and are well worth the investment.

I'm not a big fan of nonstick pans. If you cook properly, getting your pan hot enough before adding the food and then following the instructions in the recipe, food sticking to the pan is rarely an issue.

kitchen tools

A proper set of tools will make you a more efficient cook. Avoid plastic and ask Santa specifically for utensils made of stainless steel. You'll want to have the following items on hand:

colander

cooling rack

cutting board (one large, approximately 18 by 24 inches, and one small, approximately 12 by 15 inches)

grater

kitchen shears

measuring cups

measuring spoons
meat pounder
metal mixing spoon
rubber spatula
plastic storage containers
spatula
stainless steel mixing bowls
   (can't have too many)
tongs
vegetable parer
whisk
wooden spoons

the best utensils of all

Your hands are the most versatile piece of equipment in the kitchen. When you cook you'll need to get your hands involved. Chefs use their hands a lot. Your hands often work best for mixing, stirring, and coating. Don't be afraid to get messy.

knives

You don't need many. The right four knives will handle everything you need to do in this book. Make sure they're quality knives and that you keep them sharp. Easier said than done? Invest in a sharpening steel which will restore the edge to your blades with just a few deft strokes. (Ask your local butcher to demonstrate the simple sharpening technique.) Beware of "ever-sharp" knives; their serrated edges are fine for slicing, but they make chopping nearly impossible.

These are the four basic knives for your kitchen:

1. **8- or 10-inch chef's knife** (crucial to any work in the kitchen; if you had to choose only one knife, this should be it)
2. **4- or 6-inch paring knife** (for small jobs, quick cuts, and, believe it or not, paring)
3. **9- or 11-inch serrated knife** (for breads and soft tomatoes)
4. **6-inch boning knife** (has tapered end, for cutting and trimming chicken, fish, and meat)

SHOPPING

MOST OF US SHOP in supermarkets—harsh lights, endless aisles stocking a mind-boggling array of food—stores that are overwhelming and impersonal. The best way to deal with supermarkets is to get in and out as quickly as possible. Sometimes two trips to smaller grocery stores can be less debilitating than one visit to the mega-store. Try to locate a butcher and green grocer in your neighborhood. Get to know the proprietors. Shmooze. Talk loin chops, talk ripe cantaloupe. The butcher will pound your chicken breasts for you. The green grocer will steer you to the ripest fruit, the freshest vegetables. It may cost a few cents more, but it's worth having the attention and peace of mind.

how to shop

1. Select a recipe.
2. Read the ingredients list and assess what's already on hand in the pantry and fridge.
3. Make a list of what you need to buy.
4. Remember to bring the list with you into the store.
5. Once you're in the store, stay focused on what you need, get it to the car, and get out of there.

how to shop less often

The only way to save yourself a journey into the shopping abyss is to plan ahead. Decide on future menus, add to your list what you'll need to prepare them, and freeze what you can. Relocating a flank steak or boneless chicken breasts from your freezer to the fridge the day before you cook is a lot less painful than an extra trip to the supermarket.

COOKING TIPS

using a frying pan

THERE'S ALWAYS ACTION around the frying pan. You can relax in your Laz-E-Boy and read the racing results while a chicken's roasting in the oven, but when you're at the stove working the skillet, you'll be doing the Watusi.

One common mistake made in home kitchens is that people don't let the frying pan get hot enough. High heat seals in juices, develops the desired texture, and prevents food from sticking. A pan needs to sit on the gas flame for about a minute before it's ready to use. On electric stoves, a pan should be ready to use in 30 to 45 seconds after the element has reached full heat.

chopping

You have to approach chopping with the proper attitude. Don't think of it as a chore (though in France they call it "dog work") but rather as something inspiring, noble, virtuous. Here are some thoughts even the stiffest Working Stiff can use as a mantra while doing the prep work.

> *Chopping is foreplay*
> *Chopping is like the time you would spend at the travel agent's buying your tickets to Italy*
> *Chopping is like the overture to your favorite opera*
> *Chopping is like standing on line to buy tickets to a* Tony Bennett *concert*
> *Chopping is like having a winning*

bet on a horse and waiting to find
out how much it's going to pay

dicing

Slice first one direction and then the other. For example, to dice a celery stalk: Cut the stalk lengthwise into 4 or 5 thin strips. Hold these strips together and cut them across as small as you can. This principle should be applied in dicing vegetables whenever possible.

how much oil or butter should you use?

I usually recommend 2 to 3 tablespoons of oil or butter for cooking in a large skillet. You can use a bit less if you're worried about calories. Make sure you tilt the pan or use a metal spatula to spread the oil or butter over the entire bottom of the pan before adding the food.

salt & pepper—
what exactly does "to taste" mean, anyway?

A bit of salt accents the seasoning of many foods. Pepper adds bite at the finish. Together they help make much of Western cuisine resonate with flavor.

Most cookbooks (and this one is no exception) instruct you add salt and pepper "to taste." But what exactly does that mean? How *much* salt? How *much* pepper? And to whose taste? These are tough questions. My answer is a bit Zen: You'll know when you're there.

To start, try $^1/_2$ teaspoon of salt and 6 turns on the pepper grinder. Then, make sure the salt and pepper is adequately mixed into whatever you're cooking so you can taste their effect on the dish.

INSTANT DINNERS

WELCOME TO THE WORLD of Instant Dinners. Quick and efficient, these meals resemble a sting operation—you're in and you're out. No lingering. No lapsing into reverie in the kitchen as you sip your Chablis. Instant Dinners mean working quickly. They mean using high heat, in the frying pan or under the broiler. They mean limited chopping, minimal prep, a short ingredient list. The flavor comes from using first-class ingredients—such as salmon, fillet of beef, lamb chops—that are simply prepared. What adornment there is by way of sauces or spices serves as a gentle enhancement.

Timing is crucial with Instant Dinners. Since most of these entrées take about 20 minutes from start to finish, it's best to get the side dishes, such as rice or pasta, started before you begin the recipe. That way, everything will be done at the same time.

So good luck, bon appétit, and when you've become accomplished in the kitchen, which shouldn't take long, be sure to invite me for dinner.

jumbo shrimp

SERVES 2

This is the kind of meal to make after you have accomplished something big—sealed a major deal, won an important case, finally sprung for that Sinatra boxed set you've been coveting for so long. It features Goliath shrimp, Godzilla shrimp, shrimp big enough to eat other shrimp. The bread crumbs seal in the juices. The lemon teases out the flavor. Try to eat these slowly. Just try.

12 jumbo shrimp (10 to 12 per pound)

2 tablespoons olive oil

4 cloves garlic, minced

Salt and pepper to taste

$1/2$ cup unseasoned bread crumbs

$1/4$ cup freshly grated Parmesan

2 tablespoons butter

1 medium lemon, cut into wedges

Preheat the oven to 475 degrees F. To prepare the shrimp: Remove the shells, leaving the tail intact. Make a slit in the shrimp along their backs and clean out any veins.

Place the olive oil in a medium bowl and add the garlic, salt, and pepper. Add the shrimp and toss to lightly coat.

In a shallow bowl, combine the bread crumbs and Parmesan. Place each shrimp in the bread crumb mixture and turn them to lightly coat both sides. Arrange the shrimp so they aren't touching each other in an ungreased 9-by-13-inch casserole. Sprinkle them with salt and pepper. Place the pan on the center rack of the oven and bake for 8 to 9 minutes, until the shrimp are opaque in the center. Serve immediately with lemon wedges.

swift swordfish

SERVES *2*

On your way home from work, while you're stuck in traffic or crammed into a bus or train, a savory dinner of swordfish may not be the first thing that pops into your head. But once you've tried this dish, there's a good chance it will join that select pantheon of after-work reveries, right up there with martinis, taking your shoes off, and a nap.

2 tablespoons olive oil

2 (6-ounce) swordfish steaks, about 1 inch thick

1/2 cup white wine

1 cup crushed tomatoes

4 ounces white mushrooms, sliced

12 black olives, preferably Kalamata, pitted and coarsely chopped

4 tablespoons chopped fresh basil, or 1 teaspoon dried

1 teaspoon salt

Pepper to taste

Minced fresh parsley for garnish

Heat a large skillet over high heat and add the oil, spreading it so that it evenly coats the bottom of the pan. Heat the oil until it just starts smoking. Place the swordfish steaks in the pan. Cook until light brown on the bottom, about 2 minutes. Turn and sear the other side, about 2 minutes more.

Add the wine, tomatoes, mushrooms, olives, and basil, stirring gently so the vegetables are covered with sauce. Cover and cook for 5 minutes. Uncover and cook 3 to 4

minutes longer, or just until the fish is
opaque throughout. The swordfish is done
when it is firm but still slightly springy to
the touch. Don't be afraid to cut into one
of the pieces of fish to see if it's cooked
through. It's ready when it's completely
white in the middle.

Season with salt and pepper. Garnish
with the parsley and immediately serve.

note: Adding $1/2$ teaspoon anchovy
paste to the sauce along with the tomatoes
will give it a little extra sparkle.

10-minute salmon

SERVES 2

Broiled salmon is a perfect solution to a last-minute dinner. It has abundant flavor that stands up to a number of different kinds of treatments, from teriyaki to salsa. Do a quick Nutty Professor, mixing the sauce while the broiler's heating, and you'll have this dish done in a flash. Salmon freezes well if prepared properly. Freeze each piece separately, wrapped first in plastic and then in aluminum foil to preserve freshness and facilitate defrosting. This recipe can easily be doubled to serve 4.

2 (6 ounce) salmon steaks
Teriyaki Sauce, Orange-Ginger Sauce,
or Tomato Salsa (recipes follow)

Preheat the broiler. Cover the broiler pan with foil and lightly grease it with butter or vegetable oil cooking spray. Place the steaks in the pan and broil for 5 minutes. Turn the steaks carefully and broil for 4 to 5 more minutes, or until the fish is firm to the touch but still springy and slightly translucent in the center. Serve immediately topped with the sauce of your choice.

teriyaki sauce

1/4 cup soy sauce
1/4 cup sake, dry sherry, or dry white wine
1 tablespoon packed brown sugar
2 teaspoons ginger juice (see Note), or 1/2 teaspoon ground ginger
1 clove garlic, minced

Place all of the ingredients in a small saucepan and mix well. Bring the sauce to a boil just before serving.

orange-ginger sauce

1/4 cup orange juice
2 teaspoons ginger juice (see Note),
    or 1/2 teaspoon ground ginger
1 tablespoon chopped fresh cilantro
1/2 teaspoon Asian sesame oil

Place all of the ingredients in a small saucepan and mix well. Bring the sauce to a boil just before serving.

tomato corn salsa

1 plum tomato, chopped
1/2 cup canned water-packed corn,
    drained
3 scallions, green parts only, finely
    chopped
1 tablespoon freshly squeezed lime juice
1 teaspoon chili powder
1 teaspoon salt
Dash of Tabasco sauce or other hot
    sauce

Place all of the ingredients in a small bowl and mix well. Serve at room temperature alongside salmon.

note: Ginger juice is a more expedient way of dealing with fresh ginger than chopping it. Coarsely grate a 2-inch piece of unpeeled ginger. Gather the gratings into a little ball and squeeze tightly, like you would a lemon half. This should produce 2 to 3 teaspoons of potent ginger juice.

boiled rice

Several exotic kinds of white rice are now easy to find, such as basmati or the domestic version, sometimes called Texmati, and are worth trying.

3 1/2 cups water
1 1/2 cups white rice

Place the water in a 2 1/2-quart saucepan. Bring the water to a boil over high heat. Add the rice a little at a time to keep the water boiling. When all of the rice is added, cover the pan and reduce the heat to low. Simmer, covered, for 16 to 18 minutes, until the water is absorbed and the rice is just cooked through.

note: Ten-minute rice, which is precooked and packaged in plastic pouches, is worth having on hand. Place the pouches in boiling water, ten minutes later you have excellent rice. It's an expedient solution that does not sacrifice much in flavor.

fast flounder thai style

SERVES **2**

If you can't escape to an exotic locale after work, you can at least enjoy the flavor of one. The preparation here is sublimely simple for such a uniquely flavored dish. The secret is the coconut milk, which must be the unsweetened variety used for cooking, as opposed to that unctuous concoction required for piña coladas. The flounder comes out soft and fragrant, smothered with a wonderfully enticing sauce. Thai fish sauce is one of the basic pantry items and can be found in most supermarkets. Serve with Coconut Rice (see sidebar) for a scintillating Thai meal.

1 shallot

2 cloves garlic, chopped

$1/2$-inch length of fresh ginger, peeled and chopped

1 scallion, cut into 1-inch slices

$1/2$ cup canned unsweetened coconut milk

4 sprigs of fresh cilantro

1 teaspoon Thai fish sauce

2 (6-ounce) flounder fillets

Preheat the oven to 375 degrees F. Lightly grease a 9-by-13-inch casserole with butter or vegetable oil cooking spray.

Put all of the ingredients except the flounder in a blender and purée briefly. The mixture does not have to be completely smooth.

Place the flounder fillets in the casserole and pour the sauce over the fish, using your hands to make sure all of the fillets are completely coated. Bake on the center rack of the oven until the fillets are just cooked through, 8 to 10 minutes. Serve immediately.

note: Sole fillets may be substituted for flounder. Reduce the cooking time to 6 to 8 minutes.

coconut rice

SERVES 4

This quick rice is perfect served with many Asian and Caribbean dishes.

1 (15-ounce) can unsweetened coconut milk

1/2 medium onion, sliced

1 clove garlic

6 sprigs of cilantro

2 scallions, cut into 1-inch pieces

1/2 teaspoon ground ginger

1 teaspoon salt

1 1/2 cups chicken broth

1 1/2 cups rice

Put the coconut milk, onion, garlic, scallions, cilantro, ginger, and salt in the bowl of a blender and purée until just smooth. Transfer the mixture to a medium saucepan and add the broth and rice. Cover the pan and bring the liquid to a boil over medium heat. Reduce the heat to low and simmer for about 15 minutes, until the rice is just cooked through.

sole in foil

SERVES **2**

Cooking in aluminum foil ensures moist fish with lots of flavor. The only effort required is squeezing some lemon (which you might want to do anyway while making some cocktails) and folding the aluminum foil. Even the most exhausted Working Stiff should be able to handle it. This is also a very easy recipe to double or even triple. Serve with Rice Pilaf (see sidebar).

2 (6-ounce) flounder or sole fillets
1 medium lemon
Salt and pepper to taste

Preheat the oven to 400 degrees F. Lightly grease two 12-inch square pieces of aluminum foil with butter or vegetable oil cooking spray. Place 1 piece of fish in the center of each square of foil. Sprinkle some lemon juice, salt, and pepper over each fillet. Fold the top and bottom edges of the foil together, then fold each side a few times so the fish is contained in a well-sealed packet. Place the packets in a baking pan and bake on the center rack of the oven for 12 minutes.

Open the foil packets carefully and use a spatula to slide the fish onto dinner plates. Pour the drippings over the fish and serve immediately.

variations: For a hint of New Orleans flavor, sprinkle each fillet with $1/2$ teaspoon Cajun seasoning (page 68), and then top with 2 thin slices of tomato, 1 tablespoon of chopped chives, and $1/2$ teaspoon of chopped garlic before folding the foil into packets.

rice pilaf

SERVES 4

This is the rice to make when your entrée doesn't have a lot of sauce and you need the flavor of the rice to stand on its own.

2 tablespoons butter

2 shallots, minced

2 cloves garlic, minced

1¹/₂ cups rice

3¹/₂ cups chicken broth

1 teaspoon salt

Chopped fresh parsley, for garnish

Heat a large skillet over medium heat. Add the butter, spreading it so that it evenly coats the bottom of the pan. Add the shallots and garlic and cook, stirring frequently, until the shallots soften, about 2 minutes. Add the rice and stir until the grains are thoroughly coated with butter. Add the broth and salt and stir. Bring the liquid to a boil, reduce the heat to low, cover the pan, and simmer for 18 minutes, or until the rice is just cooked through. Put rice in a serving bowl or on individual plates, garnish with parsley, and serve.

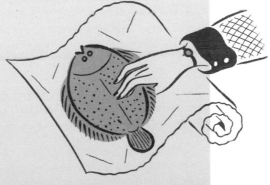

SERVES 4

This dinner has a touch of class—it's a dish you can serve to make an *impression*. The colors give it presence on the plate, and the taste is distinctive. It might be what you serve the in-laws just before you hit them up for some help with the down payment. The flattened chicken breasts cook quickly, allowing you more time at dinner to explain why your starter house should have a sauna. To make preparation even easier, pound the chicken breasts and cut the vegetables the night before, wrapping both in plastic and refrigerating.

1 cup all-purpose flour

Salt and pepper to taste

4 skinless and boneless chicken breasts, pounded to $1/4$ inch thick

3 tablespoons unsweetened butter

$1/2$ pound shiitake or white mushrooms, stemmed and cut into $1/4$-inch slices

1 (4-ounce) jar roasted red bell peppers

1 (6-ounce) jar marinated artichoke hearts, drained

2 cloves garlic, finely chopped

$1/2$ cup white wine

$1/2$ cup chicken broth

4 tablespoons chopped fresh basil, or 1 teaspoon dried

1 teaspoon salt

Freshly ground black pepper

To flatten the chicken breasts, place a 16-inch length of plastic wrap on the counter. Place 2 breasts on the plastic wrap at least 6 inches apart. Cover with another layer of plastic wrap. Whack the breasts with the flat side of a meat pounder, invoking the names of any personal or professional nemeses that might fuel your strength.

When the breasts are about half again as large and about ¹/₄ inch thick, they're ready.

Place the flour in a pie plate or shallow bowl and add salt and pepper to taste. Lay 1 chicken breast in the flour to lightly coat. Turn to coat the other side, then shake the breast gently to remove any excess flour. Place the floured breast on a large plate and repeat with the remaining 3 breasts.

Heat a large frying pan over medium-high heat and add 1 tablespoon of the butter. When it starts to sizzle, spread it to coat the bottom of the pan. Add 2 chicken breasts and cook until they are lightly browned, about 3 minutes. Turn the breasts and cook for about 2 minutes more, until they are just cooked through. Transfer to a platter.

Return the pan to the heat, add another tablespoon of butter and cook the remaining breasts. Transfer breasts to the platter and cover with aluminum foil to keep warm.

To make the sauce: Return the pan to the heat and add the remaining tablespoon of butter, the mushrooms, roasted pepper, and artichokes and cook, stirring continuously, until the vegetables soften, about 2 minutes. Add the garlic and cook 1 minute more, stirring continuously. Add the white wine and let it reduce by half, stirring continuously, about 1 minute. Add the chicken broth and basil and let the liquid reduce by half, about 90 seconds. Season with salt and pepper to taste.

To serve, place 1 chicken breast on each plate and top with the sauce.

stir-fry furioso

It's fast, furious, non-stop action. No, it's not jai alai, it's stir-fry, one of the ultimate quick, healthy, and flavorful meals. Start cooking the rice (and set a timer) before you begin stir-frying, because once you start you'll want to stay focused on the wok. Cut all of the vegetables approximately the same size so they'll cook at the same rate. You can do this the night before or while the morning coffee's brewing. Then, when you get home, dinner is just a stir-fry away. Save more time by using a bottled stir-fry sauce. Just don't tell anyone I told you.

stir-fry sauce

³/₄ cup soy sauce

³/₄ cup white wine

4 tablespoons brown sugar

2 teaspoons Asian sesame oil

1 teaspoon Chinese five-spice powder

4 tablespoons vegetable oil

1 medium onion, thinly sliced

1 medium red bell pepper, thinly sliced

4 ounces snow peas

4 ounces shiitake or white mushrooms

4 scallions, green parts only, cut into 1-inch pieces

4 cloves garlic, chopped

¹/₂-inch length of fresh ginger, finely chopped

1 pound boneless and skinless chicken breasts, thinly sliced

³/₄ cup stir-fry sauce

to make the sauce: Place the ingredients into a small bowl and stir until combined.

Place a wok or large skillet over high heat and let it get very hot, about 3 minutes. Add 2 tablespoons of the vegetable oil, the onion, red bell pepper, snow peas, and mushrooms and cook, stirring continuously, until vegetables are just cooked through, about 3 minutes. Add the scallions, garlic, and ginger and cook 1 minute more, stirring continuously. Transfer to a platter and wipe out the pan with a cloth or paper towel.

Return the pan to the heat and let it get hot, about 45 seconds. Add the remaining oil and the chicken and cook, stirring continuously, until it is just cooked through, about 2 minutes. Return the vegetables to the pan and add the sauce. Stir to completely coat everything with the sauce. Serve immediately.

variations: Substitute 1 pound thinly sliced sirloin or 1 pound large shrimp, cleaned and deveined, for the chicken. Or, to make a vegetarian stir-fry, substitute 1 cup each broccoli florets and sliced bok choy for the chicken.

note: Store any leftover sauce in a well-sealed container in the refrigerator for up to a month.

rosemary chicken breast

SERVES **2**

Marinating is one of the best friends a cook on the go can have. While you're at work, the marinade is at home working just as hard. Through various and intricate chemical processes too complicated to detail here, the oil and spices permeate the chicken so that when you cook it, it has a naturally robust flavor.

marinade

$1/4$ cup olive oil

1 tablespoon fresh or dried rosemary, minced

2 cloves garlic, crushed

1 teaspoon salt

1 teaspoon freshly ground black pepper

2 skinless and boneless chicken breasts, cut lengthwise into 1-inch strips

4 cloves garlic, minced

1 (4-ounce) jar roasted red bell peppers, drained and cut lengthwise into thin strips

$1/4$ cup dry white wine

4 tablespoons balsamic vinegar

Salt and pepper to taste

In a glass or stainless steel bowl, mix together all of the ingredients for the marinade. Add the chicken breast slices and toss gently so they are completely coated with the marinade. Cover the bowl with plastic wrap and place in the refrigerator to marinate for at least 2 hours and up to 12 hours.

Heat a medium frying pan over high heat and add 2 tablespoons of the marinade, spreading it so that it evenly coats the bottom of the pan. When the marinade just starts smoking, add the chicken breasts, garlic, and peppers and cook, stirring often, until the chicken is brown and just cooked through, 3 to 4 minutes. Add the wine and balsamic vinegar and stir until all the chicken is coated. Cook until the liquid is reduced by half, about 90 seconds. Season with salt and pepper and serve immediately.

herb-roasted new potatoes

These are the ideal accompaniment to rosemary chicken. Crispy outside, soft and warm inside, redolent with flavor—don't get me started about these potatoes. I make this recipe for four even if there are two of us. They're my weakness. Guard yours well if you ever dine at my pad.

2 pounds new potatoes, preferably Creamer or Yukon Gold, cut in half

2 tablespoons butter

1 tablespoon dried basil

1 tablespoon dried rosemary

1 teaspoon salt

Freshly ground black pepper

Preheat the oven to 375 degrees F.

Melt the butter in a small saucepan. Put the potatoes in a medium mixing bowl. Pour the melted butter over the potatoes and toss gently to lightly coat all of the potatoes. Place the potatoes in a 9-by-13-inch casserole. Sprinkle the herbs and salt and pepper, to taste, over the potatoes and bake on the center rack of the oven for about 40 minutes, until they are just cooked through. Serve immediately.

quick chicken

Here's a super-fast chicken recipe that you can embellish with two very different sauces. The first is a Cuban-style sauce with an alluring combination of citrus and spices. The second is a Chinese sauce featuring the unique flavor of black beans. The Cuban-style chicken would go well with coconut rice, the black bean sauce chicken is great with plain rice. A cold beer would be appropriate with either.

cuban garlic sauce

$1^1/_2$ cloves garlic

$^1/_2$ medium onion, sliced

$^3/_4$ cup orange juice, preferably freshly squeezed

$^1/_4$ cup freshly squeezed lime juice

$^1/_2$ teaspoon salt

$^1/_2$ teaspoon ground cumin

black bean sauce

$^1/_4$ cup soy sauce

$^1/_4$ cup chicken broth

2 tablespoons fermented black beans

1 tablespoon brown sugar

1 scallion, finely chopped

1 clove garlic, minced

$^1/_2$ cup all-pupose flour

1 tablespoon mild curry powder

$^1/_2$ teaspoon cayenne pepper

2 skinless and boneless chicken breasts, cut into 1-inch chunks

3 tablespoons vegetable oil

To make the garlic sauce, put all of the ingredients in a blender and purée just until smooth. Transfer to a small bowl and set aside.

To make the black bean sauce, put all of the ingredients for the black bean sauce in a small mixing bowl and stir together. Set aside.

Place the flour and curry or paprika in a medium bowl and stir to combine. Add the chicken pieces to the flour mixture and toss them gently so they are all lightly coated. Shake chicken pieces to remove any excess flour and transfer the chicken to a platter.

Heat a large skillet over medium-high heat and add the oil, spreading it so that it evenly coats the bottom of the pan. When the oil is hot, add the chicken pieces in a single layer. Cook until lightly browned, about 3 minutes. Use tongs to turn each piece and cook 3 minutes more, until the chicken is cooked through. Add the garlic sauce or the black bean sauce and stir to completely coat each piece of chicken. Serve immediately.

note: Fermented black beans are available in a jar in the Asian section of most supermarkets.

daiquiri

SERVES 2

These frozen drinks were purportedly invented in Cuba and, along with cigars and the mambo, they are Cuba's best known export. This strawberry version is therefore appropriate to serve with the Cuban-style chicken, but most of the Working Stiffs I know would hardly let appropriateness get between them and a frozen daiquiri.

2 cups hulled fresh or frozen strawberries
3 ounces (6 tablespoons) rum
4 tablespoons freshly squeezed lime juice
2 cups crushed ice

Put all of the ingredients in a blender and blend until smooth. Pour into tall glasses and serve immediately with a little umbrella perched at the top of the glass.

chicken fajitas

SERVES 2

This is the fastest Mexican dish around. All you do is slice, fry, roll, and eat. The simplicity of this dish could make it one of your regular weekly dinners. It can be easily doubled to accommodate another couple of Working Stiffs who happen to drop in for a meal. Just make sure they have some cold beer in hand before you let them in. Serve with Dirty Rice (page 69)which you can start cooking just before you prepare the fajitas.

2 tablespoons vegetable oil

2 boneless and skinless chicken breasts, cut into $^1/_4$-inch-thick slices

$^1/_2$ medium red bell pepper, cored, seeded and thinly sliced

$^1/_2$ medium onion, thinly sliced

2 cloves garlic, coarsely chopped

$^1/_2$ ($1^1/_4$-ounce) package taco seasoning

$^1/_2$ cup salsa

4 (9-inch) flour tortillas

1 cup grated Monterey jack or Cheddar cheese (4 ounces)

Heat a large frying pan over high heat and add the oil, spreading it so that it evenly coats the bottom of the pan. When the oil just starts smoking, add the chicken, peppers, and onions and cook, stirring continuously, until the chicken is cooked through, about 4 minutes. Add the garlic and taco seasoning and cook 1 minute more. Add the salsa and stir to completely coat the chicken and vegetables. Turn off the heat.

Heat a second large frying pan on medium-high heat. When the pan is hot, place a tortilla in the dry pan and cook until it is heated through, about 30 seconds. Turn

nd heat the other side. Remove the tortilla to
 dinner plate and place a second one in the
an. While the second tortilla is heating, place
ne-quarter of the chicken mixture in the cen-
er of the heated tortilla. Top with one-quarter
f the grated cheese. Roll up the tortilla and
lace it on a serving plate. Repeat the heating
nd rolling process with the remaining tor-
illas. Serve immediately.

variation: Substitute ½ pound
hinly sliced sirloin or ½ pound cleaned and
eveined medium shrimp for the chicken.

southwestern-style oven-fried chicken

SERVES 4

Here's a way to satisfy your craving for crispy, scrumptious fried chicken without the grease and without the effort of frying it. It's a favorite around our house. I can't wait until the kids can cook it themselves. Serve it with the Cajun Sweet Potatoes (see sidebar), which you can roast right alongside the chicken.

12 chicken drumsticks

2 eggs

1 cup unseasoned bread crumbs

1 (1 ^{1}/$_4$-ounce) package taco seasoning

Bottled chili sauce

Preheat oven to 375 degrees F. Pull the skin down to the bottom of the drumstick and cut it off with kitchen shears or a sharp knife. Set the drumsticks aside.

Beat the eggs in a wide, shallow bowl. Place the bread crumbs in a pie pan. Add the taco seasoning to the bread crumbs and mix together well. Dip a drumstick in the egg and hold it over the bowl to let the excess drip off. Set the drumstick in the bread crumbs and turn it until it is entirely coated. Place the coated drumstick on an ungreased 11-by-17-inch baking pan. Repeat with the remaining drumsticks, arranging them in the pan so they aren't touching.

Bake on the center rack of the oven for 35 to 40 minutes or until the drumsticks are golden brown on the outside and no longer pink in the center. Serve immediately with your favorite bottled chili sauce for dipping and lots of napkins.

cajun sweet potatoes

SERVES **4**

It has to be a pretty formidable entrée to relegate these potatoes to the role of side dish. If there are leftovers you can do what I do—reheat them to serve at breakfast with eggs the following day.

2 pounds sweet potatoes, peeled and cut into 1-inch-thick pieces

2 tablespoons olive oil

4 tablespoons prepared or homemade Cajun seasoning (page 68)

1 teaspoon salt

1 teaspoon freshly ground black pepper

Preheat the oven to 375 degrees F. Put the sweet potatoes in a medium bowl. Add the oil and toss the potatoes gently until they are all lightly coated. Add the Cajun seasoning, salt, and pepper and toss again.

Place the potatoes in an ungreased 9-by-13-inch casserole. Bake for 40 minutes, or until the potatoes are lightly browned and cooked through. Serve immediately.

fillet of beef with wild mushrooms

SERVES 2

This elegant meal is perfect for an intimate candlelight dinner, a prelude to conception, perhaps. Or, double the recipe for that special dinner to impress the boss (does anyone still have their boss over to dinner?). Or, if you are the boss, serve this meal to a couple of underlings to show them how the other half lives.

Salt and pepper to taste

2 (6-ounce) fillets of beef, about 1¹/₂ inches thick

1 tablespoon olive oil

1 teaspoon butter

2 shallots, finely chopped

4 ounces shiitake, portobello, or white mushrooms, stemmed and thinly sliced

¹/₂ cup white wine

¹/₂ cup heavy whipping cream

Sprinkle salt and pepper lightly on both sides of the fillets.

Place a large frying pan on high heat. Pour the olive oil in a pool in the center of the pan and place the butter in the center of the oil. When the butter starts sizzling, spread it so the oil and butter coat the bottom of the pan. Add the fillets to the pan, making sure they don't touch, and cook until they are dark brown, about 5 minutes. Turn the fillets and cook about 4 minutes more for medium-rare, 5 minutes for medium.

Remove the fillets from the pan and them let rest on a platter. Add the shallots

and mushrooms and cook, stirring continuously,
until the vegetables soften, about 2 minutes.
Add the wine and let it reduce by half over
medium-high heat, about 1 minute, while you
scrape up any bits of beef stuck to the bottom
of the pan. Add the cream and continue stirring until the sauce starts bubbling and
reduces by half, about 90 seconds. Pour the
sauce over the fillets and serve immediately.

burger bliss

Feeling blue, like you're stuck on a treadmill, looking for a cure for your Working Stiff's malaise? Maybe a burger is the answer. Cook two of these, place them between two buns, and call me in the morning.

²/₃ pound lean beef
1 tablespoon vegetable oil

Divide the beef in half and shape it into 2 large patties, about 5 inches across and ³/₄ inch thick. Do not pack the patties too tightly if you want a juicy burger.

Heat a large skillet over high heat and add the oil, spreading it so that it evenly coats the bottom of the pan. Let the pan get extremely hot (until the oil starts smoking), then add the patties. Cook them, uncovered, for 4 minutes, then turn and cook 3¹/₂ minutes more for medium-rare, 4 minutes more for medium.

variation: For cheeseburgers, put 1 slice of your favorite cheese on the burgers just after turning them. Do not make the mistake of covering the pan to help the cheese melt; this will make for soggy, steamed burgers.

superfast fudge brownies

The perfect comfort food to go
with your burgers. Brownies
always lift the spirits. Especially
these brownies. They're fast,
easy, and foolproof.

*8 tablespoons (1 stick) butter, cut into
4 pieces*

*¹/₂ cup Dutch-process unsweetened
cocoa powder*

1 cup sugar

1 teaspoon pure vanilla extract

2 extra-large eggs

³/₄ cup all-purpose flour

Preheat the oven to 325 degrees F.
Butter an 8-by-8-inch baking pan.

In a small saucepan over medium-low
heat, melt the butter with the cocoa powder,
stirring continuously until the butter is just
melted. Use a rubber spatula to transfer the
butter mixture to a large mixing bowl and let
it cool for 2 minutes. Add the sugar and vanilla
and stir with a wooden spoon until combined.
Add the eggs one at a time, stirring until each
is well combined. Add the flour and stir just
until combined. Do not overmix.

Transfer the batter to the prepared pan
and bake on the center rack of the oven for
20 minutes, or until a toothpick inserted in the
center comes out clean or with tiny crumbs on
it. Serve warm or at room temperature.

jerk skirt

SERVES 2

Skirt steak may not be part of the usual meat display at the supermarket, but the butcher will know what you're talking about. It's a cut that takes well to these strong, earthy Jamaican seasonings. You can make the jerk sauce up to three days ahead (the flavors will meld and intensify) and keep it refrigerated. Or, try one of the bottled jerk sauces, which are now readily available. Serve with Coconut Rice (page 35) and sliced fresh ripe pineapple for dessert. Put on some reggae or calypso music to get everyone in a jumpin' island mood.

jerk sauce
Makes a little more than 1 cup

²/₃ cup ketchup

4 tablespoons Pickapeppa sauce or Worcestershire sauce

2 tablespoons malt or cider vinegar

1 tablespoons allspice

1 teaspoon garlic powder

1 teaspoon brown sugar

1 teaspoon freshly ground black pepper

1 tablespoon vegetable oil

1 tablespoon butter

2 (6-ounce) skirt steaks

1 medium onion, cut in half lengthwise, and cut lengthwise again into thin slices

1 medium green bell pepper, stemmed, seeded, and cut lengthwise into thin strips

1 cup bottled or homemade jerk sauce

Put all of the ingredients for the jerk sauce in a small bowl and stir together well. Set aside.

Place a large frying pan on high heat and pour the oil in a pool in the center of the pan. Put 1 tablespoon of the butter in the center of the oil. When the butter starts sizzling, spread it so the oil and butter coat the bottom of the pan. Arrange the steaks in the pan so they aren't touching and cook until they are browned, 3 to 4 minutes. Turn and cook 2 to 3 minutes more. Remove the steaks to a platter.

Return the pan to the heat and add the onion and pepper. Cook, stirring frequently, until the vegetables soften, about 3 minutes. Add the jerk sauce and stir to coat the vegetables. Pour over the steaks and serve.

singular meat loaves

SERVES 4

The smell, the taste, the sight of a plate of meatloaf and mashed potatoes and instantly I'm a kid again, rushing through my homework so I won't miss any of that week's episode of *I Spy*. Leftover meatloaf also makes great sandwiches for a late-night snack or lunch the next day. The loaves can be prepared through step 3 the night before. Cover the pan with plastic wrap and refrigerate. The loaves may need slight adjusting to restore their shape before baking.

2 slices bread, crusts trimmed and cut into $^1/_2$-inch cubes

$^1/_2$ cup milk

1 pound lean chopped meat, such as sirloin or ground round

2 eggs

1 small onion, grated

$^1/_4$ cup barbecue sauce

1 tablespoon chili powder

1 teaspoon garlic powder

1 teaspoon Worcestershire sauce

$^1/_2$ teaspoon dried oregano

Dash of Tabasco sauce

Preheat the oven to 375 degrees F. Place the bread cubes in a medium mixing bowl. Add the milk and stir to coat all of the bread. Add the remaining ingredients and mix well, using your hands.

Shape the mixture into 4 oval loaves about 7 inches long and $3^1/_2$ inches wide at the center. Place the loaves so they aren't touching on an ungreased 9-by-13-inch casserole. Bake on the center rack of the oven for 35 to 40 minutes, or until cooked through. Cool for about 3 minutes before serving.

garlic mashed potatoes

SERVES 4

Mutt to your meatloaf's Jeff, these garlic mashed potatoes are *de rigeur*. Some like their mashed potatoes smooth and creamy. But they're not called "smooth and creamy potatoes." No! They're called mashed potatoes, because you *mash* them. They're supposed to be rough-hewn and textured, not mousse-like. The classic low-tech, handheld potato masher is the tool to use.

2 pounds russet potatoes, peeled and cut in half

4 cloves garlic, coarsely chopped

2 tablespoons butter

³/₄ cup milk

1 teaspoon salt

Put the potatoes and garlic in a large saucepan and cover with water. Bring the water to a boil over medium-high heat. Reduce the heat to medium-low and simmer the potatoes until they are just cooked through, about 20 minutes.

Drain the potatoes and transfer them to a large mixing bowl. Add the butter, milk, and salt and mash with a potato masher. Serve immediately.

variation: Add ¹/₄ cup freshly grated Parmesan to the bowl before mashing.

pork chops with orange glaze

SERVES 2

A pork chop like this doesn't come along every day. Sometimes I'm sitting at my desk in the late afternoon trying to straighten a paper clip and then restore it to its original shape (a metaphor for the existential dilemma all of us live with) when I have a surge of panic about what to make for dinner. Then I remember—it's pork chop night—and my worries cease. This dish is so very easy it puts me instantly at ease. Serve with Rice Pilaf (page 37) napped with some of the orange glaze.

$^1/_2$ cup orange juice

2 tablespoons soy sauce

1 teaspoon Asian sesame oil

1 teaspoon cornstarch

$^1/_2$ teaspoon ground ginger

2 tablespoons vegetable oil

2 center-cut loin pork chops, about 1 inch thick

Salt and pepper to taste

In a small bowl, gently whisk together the orange juice, soy sauce, sesame oil, cornstarch, and ginger until they are combined. Set aside.

Heat a large frying pan over high heat and add the oil, spreading it so that it evenly coats the bottom of the pan. When the oil just starts smoking, place the pork chops in the pan so they aren't touching. Cook until chops are browned on the bottom, about 1 minute. Turn and cook 1 minute more.

Reduce the heat to medium and cover the pan to keep the chops moist as they cook. Cook 4 minutes, turn the chops, and cover the pan again. Cook 4 to 5 minutes more, until the chops are firm but still

springy to the touch. Transfer the chops
to a platter.

Tilt the pan and spoon off and discard any excess fat. Increase the heat to
high. Add the sauce to the pan and use a
metal spatula to scrape up any bits of meat
sticking to the bottom of the pan. Once the
sauce starts to boil, reduce the heat to medium
and let the sauce simmer for 30 seconds.
Pour the sauce over the chops and serve
immediately.

pancakes

In deference to the assumption that most Working Stiffs don't have time for breakfast, I offer pancakes for dinner. And why not? Pancakes are easy and fun and may remind you of those whacky college days when you'd eat anything at any time. Serve with an egg cream and you have a dinner that's both comforting and makes up for one of the many breakfasts you've missed while climbing the ladder to success.

1 cup all-purpose flour

3 tablespoons brown sugar

1 1/4 teaspoons baking powder

Dash of ground cinnamon

Dash of salt

1 cup milk

2 tablespoons butter, melted, plus additional butter for cooking

1 egg

1 teaspoon pure vanilla extract

Real maple syrup for topping

Put the flour, brown sugar, baking powder, cinnamon, and salt in a large bowl and whisk together until well combined. Put the milk, 2 tablespoons butter, egg, and vanilla in a medium bowl and whisk together until well combined. Pour the milk mixture into the flour mixture and stir together with a wooden spoon until just combined. (It can be a bit lumpy.) Do not overmix.

Heat a large frying pan over medium-high heat and add the butter, spreading it so that it evenly coats the bottom of the pan. When the butter stops sizzling, gently pour about 1/8 cup of batter in the pan for each

ancake. Cook until the
ubbles are popping on
he surface and the pan-
akes are lightly browned
n the bottom, about 1
minute. Turn and cook 1
minute more. Serve imme-
liately with maple syrup.

egg cream

Once the nectar of Brooklyn,
New York, the egg cream has sadly
fallen out of favor. If you've never
had one, you're in for a real treat.

Milk

Chocolate syrup to taste

Cold seltzer

Fill a tall glass one-third full of milk.
Add enough chocolate to sweeten the milk and
stir well. Pour in the seltzer slowly, letting it
flow over the back of a spoon to keep the mixture from becoming too foamy. Gently stir the
egg cream. Add a bit more seltzer if desired,
and serve.

broiled lamb chops

SERVES *2*

Hey, if you're a true Working Stiff, it means you're *working*. And if you're working, it means you can afford to spring for something special once in a while. Treat yourself like you are a success and you become one, transcending the *zeitgeist* of the Working Stiff. One such reward is lamb chops—thick loin lamb chops that I ask the butcher to cut for me. I take them home, broil them, make a fast sauce, open a bottle of Zinfandel, and for that night, everything is right with the world.

shallot rosemary sauce

1 tablespoon olive oil

1 tablespoon butter

3 shallots, finely chopped

2 cloves garlic, finely chopped

$^1/_2$ cup Port or red wine

$^1/_2$ cup beef stock

1 teaspoon chopped, fresh or dried rosemary

Salt and pepper to taste

4 (3-ounce) loin lamb chops

Salt and pepper to taste

to prepare the sauce:

Place a large frying pan on high heat. Pour the oil in a pool in the center of the pan and place the butter in the center of the oil. When the butter starts sizzling, spread the oil and butter to coat the bottom of the pan. Add the shallots and cook, stirring frequently, until they are soft, about 2 minutes. Add the garlic and cook 1 minute more. Increase the heat to high, add the Port, and let it reduce by half. Add the beef broth and rosemary and continue simmering until the liquid

reduces by half. Season with salt and pepper
and set aside. Reheat the sauce just before
serving.

Preheat the broiler. Sprinkle salt
and pepper on both sides of each chop. Place
the chops on a broiler pan and broil 3 inches
from the heat for 4 to 5 minutes. Turn and
broil 4 to 5 minutes more for medium. Serve
immediately topped with the reheated sauce.

veal piccata

SERVES 2

While they proba-
bly didn't have
the Working Stiff
in mind in the
Italian country
kitchens where
they refined this
recipe, it will seem
as if it was devised
especially for you.
There aren't many
dishes simpler than
this one, and the
marriage of veal
scaloppini, white
wine, and lemon
is sublime.
Serve this after
a simple pasta
course and before
a Caesar salad for
a special meal.

¹/₂ cup all-purpose flour

1 tablespoon olive oil

1 tablespoon butter

¹/₂ pound veal scaloppini, pounded very thin

¹/₃ cup dry white wine

2 tablespoons freshly squeezed lemon juice

Salt and pepper to taste

Place the flour on a plate and spread it around.

Place a large frying pan on high heat. Pour the olive oil in a pool in the center of the pan. Place the butter in the center of the oil. When the butter starts sizzling, spread the butter and oil to coat the bottom of the pan. Quickly place a piece of veal in the flour, coating it on both sides, and shake it gently to remove any excess flour. Place it in the pan and repeat with the remaining scaloppini. Cook the scaloppini until browned, about about 1 minute. Turn and cook about 1 minute more. Transfer the scaloppini to a dinner plate.

Add the wine and lemon juice to the pan and stir with a metal spatula to release any bits of veal stuck to the bottom of the pan. Divide the scaloppini between individual plates and top with the sauce. Season with salt and pepper and serve immediately.

ONE POT DINNERS

THE IDEA HERE is quick prep and slow cooking. Because they're less frenetic, you can prepare these meals with your last few cogent synapses. They require about ten minutes or less of preparation—just a bit of razzle-dazzle before the stovetop or oven takes over. Once the dish is either simmering or baking, you can kick back, relax, finish that Haiku you're writing, darn a few socks, or check the point spread on the evening's games.

You can make the prep work for these recipes even easier by doing some of it in advance (the night before or that morning). With everything prepared, when you get home from work you'll think you're starring on a cooking show. At that point, the only way to mess up these dinners is to forget to preheat the oven.

pan-roasted salmon

Looking for a salmon you can rely on? Here it is. The trick is giving the fish a quick sauté to crisp the outside, and then baking it for a few minutes to infuse it with the earthy flavors of the herbs and garlic. Serve with Rice Pilaf (page 37) and a simple green salad. You may even want to pop open a bottle of Champagne for this meal. Not for any particular reason; maybe just because you made it through another day.

6 cloves garlic

2 scallions, green parts only

$^1/_2$ cup fresh parsley leaves

1 tablespoon fresh rosemary, or 1 teaspoon dried

1 teaspoon dried basil

2 tablespoons Dijon mustard

2 tablespoons olive oil

$^1/_2$ teaspoon salt

Pepper to taste

2 salmon steaks

$^1/_2$ cup white wine or chicken broth

Preheat the oven to 350 degrees F.

Place the garlic, scallions, parsley, and rosemary on a cutting board and chop them all together finely. Transfer to a medium bowl. Add the basil, mustard, and olive oil, and stir to combine. Spread the mixture in a thin layer over both sides of the salmon steaks.

Heat a large cast iron skillet over high heat and let it get very hot. Add the salmon steaks and cook until they are lightly browned, about 2 minutes. Turn and cook 2 minutes more.

Pour the wine into the pan, being careful not to pour it directly over the salmon, and watch out for the hot steam. Place the pan on the center rack of the oven and bake, uncovered, for 8 to 10 minutes, until the salmon is just cooked through. Serve immediately.

cajun monkfish

SERVES 4

If you ever saw a monkfish in its entirety, you might not eat the fillet. In fact, you might not eat again. It looks something like a portrait of Carol Channing painted by Hieronymus Bosch. Still, I like the flavor of monkfish, in this dish especially, with its Cajun-style spices. If you can't find monkfish in your area, either move near a better fish store or substitute snapper or mahi mahi fillets. While the fish is roasting, make some flavorful Dirty Rice (see sidebar) to go with it. You can use a commercial Cajun seasoning or mix your own.

cajun seasoning

2 tablespoons sweet Hungarian paprika

2 tablespoons chili powder

1 teaspoon garlic powder

1 teaspoon onion powder

$^1/_2$ teaspoon dried thyme

4 (5 ounce) monkfish fillets

2 tablespoons Cajun seasoning

2 tablespoons vegetable oil

2 cups canned crushed tomatoes

$^1/_2$ cup chicken broth

$^1/_2$ medium onion, finely chopped

4 cloves garlic, finely chopped

$^1/_2$ teaspoon dried basil

$^1/_2$ teaspoon dried oregano

Salt and pepper to taste

Several dashes of Tabasco sauce or other hot sauce

Combine all of the ingredients for the Cajun seasoning in a small bowl and mix well. Preheat the oven to 375 degrees F.

Sprinkle Cajun seasoning on both sides of each fillet. Heat a large cast iron skillet over high heat and add the oil, spreading it so that it evenly coats the bottom of the pan. When the oil is hot, add the fish fillets and cook until they are lightly browned, 2 to 3 minutes. Gently turn the fillets over. Add the rest of the ingredients to the pan and bring to a boil.

Place the uncovered skillet in the oven and cook for 20 to 25 minutes, or until the fish is just opaque throughout. Serve immediately.

dirty rice

This New Orleans classic goes perfectly with the Cajun Monkfish.

1 (15-ounce) can crushed tomatoes

1/2 medium onion, sliced

1 medium celery stalk, cut into 1-inch pieces

1/2 medium green bell pepper, cut into 1-inch pieces

2 cloves garlic

2 scallions, cut into 1-inch pieces

1 tablespoon chili powder

1/2 teaspoon ground cumin

1 teaspoon salt

1 tablespoon butter

1 1/2 cups rice

1 1/2 cups chicken broth

Put the tomatoes, onion, celery, bell pepper, garlic, scallions, chili powder, cumin, and salt in a blender and purée just until smooth. Set aside.

Heat a large skillet over high heat and add the butter, spreading it so that it evenly coats the bottom of the pan. Add the rice and stir until the grains are thoroughly coated with the butter. Add the tomato mixture and chicken broth and bring the liquid to a boil. Reduce the heat, cover the pan, and simmer for 20 minutes, or until the rice is cooked through. Serve immediately.

providence fish stew

SERVES 4

Inspired by the Portuguese community in Providence, I first made this dish while I was in college, inviting several friends to share it with me. So grateful were they for a home-cooked meal, they arrived bearing sumptuous desserts, great loaves of bread, and bottles of wine with corks instead of screw tops. (Now I enjoy it with an Australian Shiraz.) Like many one-pot meals, this one has what might at first seem a daunting list of ingredients. But if you do a quick Sherlock Holmes on the recipe, you'll see the preparation is, well, elementary.

1 tablespoon olive oil

4 ounces chorizo or other smoked sausage, thinly sliced

1 medium onion, chopped

2 medium celery stalks, thinly sliced

1 medium red bell pepper, cored, seeded, and coarsely diced

1 cup diced peeled sweet potato

4 cloves garlic, minced

1 (28-ounce) can crushed tomatoes

$^1/_2$ cup dry red wine

2 cups chicken broth

1 teaspoon sweet paprika

1 teaspoon dried basil

1 teaspoon dried oregano

$1^1/_2$ pounds fish fillets (haddock, cod, or flounder), cut into 1-inch thick pieces

$^1/_2$ pound medium shrimp, shelled and deveined

Salt and pepper to taste

Place a large saucepan over medium-high heat and add the oil, spreading it so that it evenly coats the bottom of the pan. Add the sausage, onion, celery, pepper, and

eet potato and cook, stirring frequently,
til the vegetables soften, about 4 minutes.
d the garlic and cook 1 minute more. Add
e tomatoes, wine, chicken broth, paprika,
sil, and oregano and stir. Increase the heat
high and bring the liquid to a boil, then
luce the heat and simmer, partially covered,
20 minutes.

Add the fish and shrimp and continue
mering until they are cooked through,
out 7 minutes. Season with salt and pepper.
rve immediately with a crusty French bread.

paella rapido

SERVES 4

This is an abbreviated but no less flavorful version of the classic Spanish dish. Granted, paella in a Barcelona restaurant made with shrimp and fish that just hours before were swimming in the Mediterranean will probably taste better. But as a quick junket to paella-ville isn't on the commute home for most of us, this version will do. Don't see the length of the ingredient list as a potential snafu. Everything winds up in one pot and cooks up splendidly. Serve with sangría to make the evening more authentic.

3 cups chicken broth

Pinch of saffron

2 tablespoons extra-virgin olive oil

4 chicken thighs

1 medium onion, finely chopped

4 cloves garlic, finely chopped

4 ounces smoked sausage, cut into
  $1/2$-inch-thick pieces

$1 1/2$ cups rice

1 (28-ounce) can whole tomatoes,
  drained

1 (4-ounce) jar roasted red bell peppers,
  drained

12 ounces medium shrimp (about 20),
  cleaned and deveined

1 cup frozen peas

Preheat oven to 350 degrees F.

Heat the chicken broth in a medium saucepan. Add the saffron and simmer over low heat while you prepare the rest of the dish.

Heat a large cast iron skillet over high heat and add 1 tablespoon of the oil, spreading it so that it evenly coats the bottom of the pan. When the oil is hot, add the

icken thighs and cook until they are light-
brown on the bottom, 3 to 4 minutes.
urn and brown the other side, 3 to 4 min-
:es. Transfer the thighs to a platter.

Add the remaining 1 tablespoon of
l to the pan. Add the onions and cook,
irring frequently, until they soften, about
minutes. Add the garlic, sausage, and rice
d cook 1 minute more, stirring continuously,
til the rice is lightly coated with oil.

Return the chicken to the pan and
d the tomatoes, roasted peppers, and
rimp. Pour the hot chicken broth into the
n and carefully stir everything together.
ver the pan and bake on the center rack of
e oven for 45 minutes, or until the chicken
cooked through. Stir in the frozen peas
ring the last 5 minutes of cooking. Serve
mediately.

note: Smoked turkey or chicken
usage both work fine for this dish. If you
n't find smoked sausage, 4 ounces of diced
oked ham will also work.

sangría

Wine with a touch of sugar and lots of fruit, served cold, can really help ease some of the cares of the Working Stiff.

1 bottle (750 ml) dry red wine

2 tablespoons light brown sugar, or to taste

1 cup freshly squeezed orange juice

1 orange, thinly sliced

1 lemon, thinly sliced

1 apple, cut into 1-inch dice

1 mango or papaya, peeled, seeded, and diced

12 ice cubes

Combine the wine and brown sugar in a large pitcher and stir to dissolve. Add the orange juice and the fruits. Let the mixture sit at room temperature for at least 30 minutes and up to 1 hour for the fruit to macerate. Add the ice, stir well, and serve in tall glasses.

chicken parmesan

SERVES 4

This dish is as American as apple pie. It's also the perfect family meal because everyone seems to like it. While you're preparing the chicken, put some water on to boil for pasta to accompany it. Cook the pasta while the chicken is in the oven. Leftover chicken Parmesan is great reheated the next day for lunch. Or, put the breasts on some crusty Italian bread and enjoy as a sub sandwich.

1 egg

³/₄ cup unseasoned bread crumbs

2 tablespoons freshly grated Parmesan cheese

Salt and pepper to taste

4 boneless and skinless chicken breasts

2 tablespoons olive oil

³/₄ cup store-bought or homemade tomato sauce

4 ounces mozzarella cheese, cut into thin slices

Preheat the oven to 375 degrees F.

Beat the egg in a shallow bowl. Place the bread crumbs and Parmesan in a pie pan, add salt and pepper, and mix together. Dip chicken breast into the beaten egg, and then hold it above the bowl to let the excess drip off. Place the chicken breast in the bread crumbs and lightly coat each side. Place the coated breast on a plate and repeat with the remaining 3 breasts.

Heat a large frying pan over high heat and add the oil, spreading it so that it evenly coats the bottom of the pan. When the oil is hot, add the chicken breasts, arranging them in the pan so they aren't

uching. Cook the breasts until they are
ghtly browned, 1 to 2 minutes. Turn and
own the other side, 1 to 2 minutes more.
urn off the heat.

Spoon about 2 tablespoons of tomato
uce on each breast and top with a few slices
the mozzarella cheese. Place the pan in the
en on the center rack and bake for 15 min-
es, or until the breasts are cooked through
d are firm but springy to the touch. Serve
mediately.

deluxe chicken breast

SERVES 2

My brother-in-law laid this little gem of a recipe on me. His company, Deluxe Motion Picture Catering, might make 350 of these on a given day, depending on how many extras there are on the set. The "deluxe" part of the preparation is that you place the cheese-tomato filling under the chicken skin. It's actually pretty easy, the same basic technique as when, in summer camp, you Frenched your bunkmate's sheets. Serve with wild rice, which should be done just in time for dinner if you start cooking it when you begin preparing the chicken.

2 ounces herbed Boursin cheese (see Note)

2 tablespoons chopped sun-dried tomatoes packed in oil

2 chicken breasts, bone and skin on

1 tablespoon olive oil

1 tablespoon butter

Preheat the oven to 375 degrees F.

Place the cheese and sun-dried tomatoes in a small bowl and mix them together until fully combined. Pull back the skin on the chicken breasts and divide the cheese mixture evenly over the flesh. Put the skin back in place over the cheese mixture and secure it on each side with a toothpick.

Place a large cast iron skillet on high heat. Pour the olive oil in a pool in the center of the pan and place the butter in the center of the oil. When the butter starts sizzling, spread it so the oil and butter coat the bottom of the pan. Place the breasts in the pan skin side down and cook until they are light browned, about 2 minutes. Turn the breasts and put the pan in the oven on the center rack. Roast for 30 minutes, until the chicken is just cooked through. Serve immediately.

note: Boursin is a brand of soft, herbed cheese available in the dairy section of most supermarkets.

wild rice

If you have the time to cook wild rice, try it as a flavorful alternative to white or brown rice.

3 cups water

1 teaspoon salt

1 1/2 cups wild rice

Place the water and salt over high heat in a medium heavy-bottomed saucepan and bring to a boil. Stir in the rice. When the water returns to a boil, immediately reduce the heat to low, cover the pan, and simmer the rice for 45 to 50 minutes, until it has doubled in size and is soft but still has a slightly chewy center (al dente). Serve immediately.

chicken curry in a hurry

SERVES *2*

I love a good curry, especially when it's made in one pan. This recipe has both things going for it. The addition of the apple softens the curry by adding a touch of sweetness to the sauce. As the curry cooks, it fills the house with an exotic aroma and soon the stresses of the day drift away in a haze of spices. Or not. Anyway, it's worth a try. Start cooking the rice (page 33) when the chicken begins simmering and it will be done in time to serve with the curry.

1 tablespoon olive oil

1 tablespoon butter

2 chicken breasts

1 medium onion, cut in half lengthwise then cut lengthwise again into thin slices

1 medium Granny Smith apple, peeled, cored, and cut into thin slices

1 cup peeled baby carrots

$^1/_2$ pound white mushrooms, thinly sliced

3 cloves garlic, finely chopped

$^1/_2$-inch length of fresh ginger, finely chopped

2 tablespoons curry powder

$^1/_2$ cup lowfat sour cream

$^1/_2$ cup chicken broth

Place a large frying pan on high heat. Pour the olive oil in a pool in the center of the pan and place the butter in the center of the oil. When the butter starts sizzling, spread it so the oil and butter coat the bottom of the pan. Add the chicken breasts and cook until they are lightly browned, 3 4 minutes. Turn and brown the other side,

to 4 minutes. Transfer the breasts to a plat-
er. Pour out and discard the excess fat and
return the pan to the stove

Reduce the heat to medium. Add the
onion, apple, carrots, and mushrooms and cook,
stirring frequently, until they just begin to
soften, about 3 minutes. Add the garlic, ginger, and curry powder and cook 2 minutes
more, stirring continuously. Don't worry if the
curry powder starts sticking to the bottom of
the pan. Add the sour cream and chicken broth
and stir well. Place the chicken breasts in the
pan and spoon the vegetables over them. Cover
the pan and reduce the heat to the lowest set-
ting. Simmer for 30 to 35 minutes, until the
chicken is cooked through. Serve over hot rice.

fast turkey chili

SERVES 4 TO 6

Chili isn't usually one of those dishes you plan to make. It just sort of comes to mind—"Oh, I know, how about chili?" It's like renting *Casablanca*; it wasn't the movie you wanted when you walked in the video store, but once you're watching it, you're quite content. This chili is perfect when you want to throw together an impromptu meal for some friends. It also makes great left-overs. The turkey makes this a little lighter than most chilis. Serve with rice (page 33), which you can start cooking once the chili is simmering.

1 tablespoon vegetable oil

1 medium onion, chopped

1 medium red bell pepper, cored, seeded, and cut into ¹/₂-inch dice

1 medium green bell pepper, cored, seeded and cut into ¹/₂-inch dice

2 medium celery stalks, thinly sliced

1 pound lean ground turkey

4 cloves garlic, minced

¹/₄ cup mild chili powder

1 (28-ounce) can crushed tomatoes

1 (15-ounce) can pinto beans, drained

1 teaspoon dried oregano

1 teaspoon salt

1 (9-ounce) box frozen corn

Heat a large pot over high heat and add the oil, spreading it so that it evenly covers the bottom of the pot. When the oil is hot, add the onion, bell peppers, celery, and turkey and cook, stirring often, until the turkey has lost its pinkness and is cooked through, about 2 minutes. Add the garlic and cook 1 minute. Add the chili powder and cook, stirring continuously, for 1 minute. Add the tomatoes, beans, oregano, and salt and stir well to combine.

Bring the chili to a boil. Reduce the
eat to low and simmer, partially covered,
r 20 minutes, stirring occasionally. Add the
ozen corn, stir to combine, and cook 10
inutes more. Serve over rice.

chicken with porcini mushrooms

SERVES 2

Did you know that cooking with dried mushrooms is just as easy as making instant coffee and considerably easier than trying to grow sea monkeys? Try this: When you first wake up, before you start trying to retrieve something to wear from the hamper, go directly into the kitchen and put a handful of porcini into a bowl of water. *Voila!* You've mastered dried mushrooms. A day of soaking and they're ready to be sautéed that night.

¹/₂ ounce porcini or other dried
  mushrooms (such as chanterelles
  or morels)
1¹/₂ cups lukewarm water
2 tablespoons olive oil
1 whole chicken, cut into 6 pieces
1 large onion, thinly sliced
2 russet potatoes, cut into 1-inch-thick piec
1 cup dry white wine
Salt and pepper to taste

At least 1¹/₂ hours before cooking, put the mushrooms into a small bowl with the water. Stir until the mushrooms are covered. Let them soak until they are quite soft

Heat a 4-quart pot over medium-high heat and add the oil. Add the chicken and onion and cook, stirring occasionally until the chicken is browned, about 10 minutes.

Remove the mushrooms from their liquid without disturbing any grit that might have settled on the bottom. Add the mushrooms to the pot along with the potatoes, wine, basil, salt, and pepper and bring to a boil. Cover the pan, reduce heat to low, and simmer for 25 minutes, or until cooked through. Serve immediately.

steak in a brown paper bag

SERVES 2

There may have been occasions when you've wanted to put a brown paper bag over your head after you've cooked something. Here you actually use it to prepare the steak. Sounds weird, but I've found this to be the best way to cook a steak short of barbecuing it. Take the steak out of the refrigerator 15 minutes or so before you cook it to bring it to room temperature. Serve with Cajun Sweet Potatoes (page 49), which you can roast in the same oven as the steak.

$1^3/_4$-pound boneless shell steak, about $2^1/_2$ inches thick

2 tablespoons olive oil

4 cloves garlic, minced

Salt and pepper to taste

$^1/_2$ cup unseasoned bread crumbs

Preheat the oven to 375 degrees F.

Rub both sides of the steak with olive oil. Press on the garlic, season with salt and pepper, and press the bread crumbs on both sides of the steak. Place the steak in the bottom of a brown paper bag and fold the bag up tightly. Put the bag in a 9-by-13-inch casserole seam side down and bake on the center rack of the oven for 35 minutes for medium-rare; cook 3 minutes more for medium. Let the steak rest for about 2 minutes before slicing and serving.

stuffed flank steak

SERVES 4

I used to watch the butchers in Boston's Haymarket Square prepare this stuffed flank steak for the women from the Italian North End. Ask your butcher to butterfly the flank steak for you. Not only will he be happy to accommodate you, but he'll no doubt be impressed with your culinary acumen. Assemble the flank steak the night before or that morning and you can put it in the oven when you get home from work.

1 1/2- to 2-pound flank steak, butterflied

1 tablespoon olive oil

1 medium onion, cut in half lengthwise, and then thinly sliced lengthwise

1 medium red bell pepper, cored, seeded, and thinly sliced lengthwise

1/2 medium fennel bulb, peeled and thinly sliced (see Note page 99)

2 cloves garlic, finely chopped

1/4 cup unseasoned bread crumbs

4 slices prosciutto or thinly sliced smoked ham

1 teaspoon dried oregano

2 tablespoons freshly grated Parmesan

1 cup grated Gruyère, Edam, or fontina cheese (about 2 ounces)

Preheat the oven to 350 degrees F. Lightly grease a 9-by-13-inch casserole with vegetable oil cooking spray.

Place the flank steak on a cutting board and spread it flat.

Heat a large frying pan over high heat and add the oil, spreading it so that it evenly coats the bottom of the pan. When the oil is hot, add the onion, pepper, and fennel and cook, stirring frequently, until the vegetables soften, about 3 minutes. Add the garlic and cook 1 minute more. Transfer the vegetables to a medium bowl, add the bread crumbs, and stir to combine.

Arrange the prosciutto slices over the flank steak. Spread the vegetable mixture over the prosciutto. Sprinkle the oregano and the two cheeses over the top. Roll the steak up lengthwise and place it in the casserole seam side down. Bake on the center rack of the oven for 50 to 55 minutes for medium-rare. Let the meat rest for a minute or two before cutting it into 2-inch slices.

frittata rustica

SERVES **6**

Friends are coming for dinner in an hour, but you're not panicked, not whirling dervish-like around the stove, frantically getting the food ready. You're not even in the kitchen. Why? Because you've already set out an assortment of antipasti you got from from a local gourmet shop— olives, breadsticks, cherry tomatoes, kirby cucumber spears, caponata spread, focaccia. And you know the frittata you're making will only take a few minutes, so there's no reason to worry.

10 *extra-large eggs*

1 *(4-ounce jar) roasted red bell peppers, drained and thinly sliced*

1 *(4-ounce jar) artichoke hearts, drained and chopped*

4 *tablespoons chopped oil-packed sun-dried tomatoes*

4 *scallions, cut into $^{1}/_{2}$-inch pieces*

1 *cup (about 4 ounces) grated hard cheese, such as Cheddar, pecorino Romano, fontina, or Gruyère*

1 *tablespoon olive oil*

1 *tablespoon butter*

Preheat the broiler and adjust the oven rack to the center position in the oven.

Beat the eggs in a medium bowl. Add the peppers, artichokes, sun-dried tomatoes, scallions, and cheese and stir to combine.

Place a 10-inch cast iron skillet on high heat. Pour the olive oil in a pool in the center of the pan and place the butter in the center of the oil. When the butter starts sizzling, spread it so the oil and butter coat the bottom and halfway up the sides of the pan. Add the egg mixture and cook, stirring continuously, until the eggs are almost set. Use a metal spatula to

scrape the eggs from the bottom of the pan
and incorporate them into the mixture.

Transfer the pan to the center rack of
the oven and broil for 1 to 2 minutes, until
the top is nicely browned. Remove the pan
from the oven and let the frittata rest in the
pan for about 2 minutes before removing it.

To remove the frittata, run a metal
spatula around the edge of the pan and
underneath the frittata to loosen it. Tilt the
pan (remember that the handle is still hot)
and use the spatula to ease it out onto a
serving platter. Cut into 6 wedges and serve.

note: For a tasty variation, add
2 ounces of diced smoked ham, cooked bacon,
or prosciutto to the egg mixture before
cooking.

sicilian vegetable stew

SERVES 4

Someday you may retire from the Working Stiff life and find yourself in a little town in Sicily. You return from the market and as the sun sets over the Ionian Sea, you cook dinner, letting the ocean breezes blend with the sumptuous aroma of this savory stew. But until then, you'll have to prepare it in your Working Stiff's kitchen. It's a great dish to cook in advance and freeze so it's ready for reheating when you get home from work. Serve with couscous (see sidebar), which, because it cooks so quickly, should be prepared when the stew is finished.

3 tablespoons olive oil

1 medium eggplant, peeled and cut into 1-inch cubes

1 medium onion, finely chopped

1 medium red bell pepper, cored, seeded, and cut into 1-inch dice

2 small zucchini, trimmed and cut into $^1/_2$-inch-thick rounds

1 (6-ounce) jar artichoke hearts, drained

3 cloves garlic, minced

1 (28-ounce) can crushed tomatoes

12 green olives, pitted and chopped

4 tablespoons chopped fresh basil, or 1 teaspoon dried

2 tablespoons chopped fresh parsley

1 teaspoon dried oregano

$^1/_2$ teaspoon ground cumin

$^1/_2$ teaspoon cayenne pepper

Salt and pepper to taste

Place a 6-quart pot on high heat and add the oil, spreading it so it evenly coats the bottom of the pan. When the oil is just smoking, add the eggplant and cook, stirring frequently, until it begins to brown, about 3 minutes. Add the onion, red bell pepper, and

ucchini and cook, stirring frequently, until
he vegetables soften slightly, about 3 min-
tes. Add the artichokes and garlic and cook
minute more. Add the tomatoes, olives,
asil, parsley, oregano, cumin, and cayenne
nd stir to combine.

Bring the liquid to a boil, and then
educe the heat to medium-low and simmer,
ncovered, for 12 minutes. Season with salt
nd pepper. Serve hot, spooned over couscous.

COUScous

Couscous' distinctive
flavor and ease of
preparation make it
an excellent side
dish. Couscous will
become gummy if
you overcook it. Just
follow the recipe
carefully and it'll
come out great.

2 cups chicken broth

1 tablespoon butter

1 cup couscous

Put the chicken broth
and butter in a large
saucepan and bring to a
boil over high heat. Add
the couscous slowly, stirring continuously. As soon
as the liquid returns to a
boil, cover the pan and
reduce the heat to low.
Simmer for exactly 1
minute, then remove the
pan from the heat. Cover
the pan and let the cous-
cous sit for 5 minutes.
Fluff the couscous with a
fork before serving.

vegetarian skillet chilaquiles

This is a Mexican-style lasagna—layers of chili sauce, beans, tortilla chips, and cheese cooked together in a skillet. It would be perfect to serve at a small, informal dinner party on a Friday to help you make a jovial segue into the weekend. Bring the pan to the table along with some bowls of sour cream and guacamole, and dish it up as you and your friends swap stories of computer mishaps and copier jams. A large green salad is all you really need to complete this meal.

2 tablespoons vegetable oil

1 medium green bell pepper, cored, seeded, and cut into $^1/_2$-inch dice

1 medium onion, thinly sliced

2 small zucchini, cut into $^1/_4$-inch rounds

1 ($1^1/_4$-ounce) package taco seasoning

1 tablespoon mild chili powder

1 (28-ounce) can crushed tomatoes

1 (16-ounce) jar salsa

1 (15-ounce) can red beans, drained

2 cups grated Cheddar or Monterey Jack cheese (about 8 ounces)

1 teaspoon salt

6 ounces tortilla chips

Preheat the oven to 350 degrees F.

Heat a large cast iron skillet over high heat and add the oil, spreading it so that it evenly coats the bottom of the pan. When the oil is just smoking, add the pepper, onion, and zucchini and cook, stirring frequently, until the vegetables soften, about 3 minutes. Add the taco seasoning and chili powder and cook for 1 minute, stirring continuously. Add the crushed tomatoes, salsa,

d beans and bring the
ixture to a boil. Reduce
e heat to low and simmer,
ncovered, for 10 minutes,
irring occasionally to keep
from scorching. Turn off
e heat.

Use a ladle to transfer
l but ½ inch of the mix-
re to a large bowl.
prinkle ¼ of the grated
eese over the layer of
uce remaining in the pan.
reak a handful of tortilla
ips into large pieces and
range them over the
eese. Cover the chips
ith a layer of sauce, top
ith one-quarter of the
eese, then break up
other handful of chips
d layer them over the
eese. Repeat, using the
maining chips and sauce.
over the final layer of
uce with the remaining
eese. Place the pan on the
enter rack of the oven and
ake for 25 minutes. Serve
mmediately.

note: Baked tortilla
ips and reduced-fat cheese
ay be used to help lower
e fat content of this dish.

chocolate pecan pie

SERVES 6

Though nuts and chocolate
are often paired in Mexican
cooking, this pie transcends any
one cuisine. I owe the recipe to
my friend Chris, a true gourmand,
whose mission is to search out
simple yet indulgent recipes to
satisfy his desires.

10 tablespoons (1 stick plus 2 tablespoons) butter, softened

¾ cup packed brown sugar

3 extra-large eggs

1 cup dark corn syrup

1 cup pecan halves

1½ cups (6 ounces) bittersweet chocolate,
chopped into chip-sized pieces

1 teaspoon pure vanilla extract

1 (9-inch) frozen pie crust

Preheat the oven to 450 degrees F.

Put the butter in a large bowl and stir
in the sugar with a wooden spoon until smooth,
about 3 minutes. Beat the eggs in one at a time,
until each is incorporated. Add the remaining
ingredients. Pour the filling into the crust.

Bake on the center rack of the oven for
10 minutes. Reduce the heat to 350 degrees F
and bake for 30 to 35 minutes more, until the
pie is set and a toothpick inserted in the center
comes out clean. Cool before serving.

PASTA

PASTA ALLOWS YOU to get dinner on
the table in the 32 minutes it takes to fill a
pot with water (assuming average water pres-
sure), bring the water to a boil, and cook the
pasta. The sauces I've included are designed to
be prepared in this brief amount of time. You
can make the sauce while the water is boiling,
if you like. Or prepare the sauce ahead of time
and freeze it. Many of the sauces can easily be
made in advance, doubled, and frozen in plastic
containers. Dinner, then, is just a matter of
boiling the pasta and defrosting the sauce.
With pasta as a main course, you usually only

need to prepare soup or a large salad to round out the meal.

Many novices in the kitchen discover they are quite comfortable cooking pasta. Many of the standard kitchen anxieties concerning preparation are absent with pasta. It's easy to tell when it's done (you lift a piece from the pot, let it cool a few seconds, and taste it). There is little ambiguity about how to serve it (the pasta goes on the bottom, the sauce on the top). And best of all, you like it, your friends like it, your Significant Other likes it. If you don't have a Significant Other, preparing a luscious bowl of pasta for a date will set you on the right track. And if it doesn't work out, at least you had a decent meal. (Try to get your date to do the dishes before saying good night).

Most of these recipes call for dried pasta, which takes between 7 and 12 minutes to cook, depending on the thickness. Figure on 4 to 5 servings per pound. Fresh pasta is usually more expensive, cooks more quickly (in 2 to 3 minutes), and makes about 3 servings per pound. There isn't too much difference between dried and fresh pasta once they're cooked, though because fresh pasta is so soft, it is harder to cook it al dente. Whether using fresh or dried pasta, be sure you cook it in plenty of water. Your 8-quart pasta pot should be two-thirds full of rapidly boiling water before you add the pasta.

spaghetti with portobellos, prosciutto & cream

SERVES *2*

Pasta and cream appropriately combined is a sublime experience. And, being a Working Stiff, I'm on the lookout for any opportunity to cram a little more of the sublime into my life.

6 ounces dried spaghetti

1 tablespoon olive oil

1 tablespoon butter

1 portobello mushroom (about 4 ounces), stemmed, cut in half, and thinly sliced, or 4 ounces white mushrooms

3 shallots, finely chopped

³/₄ cup heavy whipping cream

2 ounces prosciutto or Westphalian ham, cut into 1-inch dice

3 tablespoons freshly grated Parmesan

Salt and pepper to taste

Fill an 8-quart pot two-thirds full of water and bring it to a boil over high heat. Add the spaghetti and stir well to keep it from sticking. Boil the pasta until it is cooked through, 8 to 10 minutes.

Meanwhile, heat a large skillet on high heat. Pour the oil in a pool in the center of the pan. Place the butter in the center of the oil. When the butter starts sizzling, spread it so the oil and butter coat the bottom of the pan. Add the mushrooms and cook, stirring continuously, until the mushrooms soften, about 4 minutes. Add the shallots and cook 2 minutes more. Add the cream and prosciutto

nd stir until the cream reduces by half,
bout 3 minutes. Stir in the Parmesan and
eason with salt and pepper.

Drain the pasta in a colander and
ransfer it to a large pasta bowl. Use a rub-
er spatula to scrape the sauce over the
asta and toss gently so the noodles are
ghtly coated. Serve immediately.

linguini with meat sauce & fennel

SERVES 4

This is a hearty pasta. An intrepid pasta. Pasta with aplomb. Served with a simple green salad, this will be your whole meal. It takes just a tad longer to make than most of the other sauces, but since it tastes even better after a night or two in the refrigerator, consider preparing it in advance. This way, when you call to say you'll be home too late to make dinner, your Significant Other will have an easy time of it.

2 ounces dried linguini

1 tablespoon olive oil

$^1/_3$ pound sweet Italian sausage, casing removed

$^1/_3$ pound lean ground beef

1 medium onion, finely chopped

$^1/_2$ medium fennel bulb, peeled and diced (see Note)

4 cloves garlic, minced

$^1/_2$ cup dry red wine or beef broth

1 (28-ounce) can crushed tomatoes

1 tablespoon chopped fresh rosemary, or 1 teaspoon dried

4 tablespoons chopped fresh basil, or 1 teaspoon dried

Salt and pepper to taste

Freshly grated Parmesan, for garnish

Heat a large skillet over high heat and add the oil, spreading it so that it evenly coats the bottom of the pan. When the oil is just smoking, add the sausage and beef and cook until the meat loses its pinkness, about 4 minutes. Break the sausage meat up with spoon while it is cooking. Use a slotted spoon to transfer the meat to a bowl. Pour out and discard the fat from the pan.

Fill an 8-quart pot two-thirds full of water and bring it to a boil over high heat. Add the linguini and stir to keep it from sticking. Cook the pasta until it is al dente, 8 to 10 minutes.

Meanwhile, return the skillet to the stove and lower the heat to medium. Add the onion and fennel and cook, stirring continuously, until the onion softens, about 4 minutes. Add the garlic and cook 1 minute more. Return the meat to the pan, add the wine or broth, and cook until the liquid reduces by half, about 1 minute. Add the tomatoes, rosemary, and basil and bring to a boil. Reduce the heat to medium-low and simmer the sauce until the pasta is done.

Drain the pasta in a colander and transfer it to a large pasta bowl. Pour the sauce over the pasta and serve topped with a generous sprinkling of Parmesan.

notes: Equal amounts of ground turkey and turkey sausage can be substituted for the ground beef and Italian sausage. For a vegetarian version, substitute 1 medium eggplant, peeled and cut into 1-inch cubes, for the meat.

To dice the fennel, peel off any outside layers that are discolored. Trim away the root and cut the bulb in half lengthwise. Place the bulb cut side down on a cutting board and cut it lengthwise into thin slices. Cut the slices crosswise into $1/4$-inch dice.

lazy man's lasagna

SERVES 4

Where regular lasagna is a complicated and involved procedure, this version requires minimal synapses: yet it manages to provide the essence of the lasagna experience: pasta, oozing melted mozzarella, tomato sauce. I like to prepare this dish with fresh mozzarella, which melts more easily than the packaged kind. Since you exerted so little effort making the entrée, you should have enough wherewithal to whip up a dessert, such as a Lemon Pie (see sidebar).

12 ounces dried ziti

3 tablespoons olive oil

4 ounces white mushrooms, thinly sliced

2 shallots, finely chopped

3 cloves garlic, minced

1/2 cup chicken broth or dry white or red wine

1 (28-ounce) can whole tomatoes

4 tablespoons chopped fresh basil, or 1 teaspoon dried

Salt and pepper to taste

2 cups grated fresh mozzarella (8 ounces)

1/4 cup freshly grated Parmesan

Fill an 8-quart pot two-thirds full of water and bring it to a boil over high heat. Add the ziti and stir to keep it from sticking. Cook the pasta until it is al dente, about 8 minutes.

Meanwhile, heat a large skillet over medium-high heat and add the oil, spreading it so that it evenly coats the bottom of the pan. Add the mushrooms and shallots and cook, stirring continuously, until they are soft, about 3 minutes. Add the garlic and cook 1 minute more. Add the chicken broth and cook, stirring frequently, until the liquid is reduced by half, about 1 minute. Add the tomatoes and their juice and break them up with a wooden spoon. Cook until the sauce thickens slightly, about 5 minutes. Add the basil, salt, and pepper and stir to combine. Simmer the sauce on low heat until ready to use.

Drain the ziti in a colander and immediately transfer one-third of it to a large pasta bowl. Sprinkle half of the grated mozzarella over the pasta. Add another third of the pasta on top of the mozzarella and cover this layer with the remaining mozzarella. Place the remaining pasta on the cheese and pour the sauce over it. Sprinkle the Parmesan over the sauce, toss gently, and serve immediately.

variations: To gently enhance this dish, 1 cup of diced smoked sausage or leftover cooked chicken can be added to the sauce. For another variation, cremini or shiitake mushrooms can replace the white mushrooms.

lemon pie

SERVES 6 TO 8

The ratio of kudos to time spent in preparation is outstanding with this recipe.

4 egg yolks

1 (15-ounce) can condensed milk

³/₄ cup freshly squeezed lemon juice (about 6 lemons)

1 prepared graham cracker crust

Preheat oven to 350 degrees F.

Put the egg yolks and condensed milk into a medium mixing bowl and blend with a handheld electric mixer on medium-high speed until the mixture lightens, about 3 minutes. With the mixer running, slowly add the lemon juice until it is entirely incorporated. Pour the mixture into the prepared crust. Bake on the center rack of the oven for 22 minutes, or until it is completely set. Remove the pie from the oven and let it cool for an hour.

fettucini with smoked salmon

SERVES *2*

Simple, quick, and elegant. Those words get thrown around quite a bit with regard to recipes, but this one is the real deal. Prepare this dish as the center-piece for a romantic dinner for two. Don't even wait for a spe-cial occasion. Just any time you want to be reminded of the good in life. Serve with Champagne.

12 ounces fresh fettucini, or
    6 ounces dried
1 tablespoon butter
2 shallots, finely chopped
4 ounces white mushrooms, thinly sliced
³/₄ cup heavy whipping cream
3 ounces smoked salmon, coarsely
    chopped
Salt and pepper to taste
2 tablespoons freshly grated Parmesan,
    for garnish
Chopped fresh parsley, for garnish

Fill an 8-quart pot two-thirds full of water and bring it to a boil over high heat. Add the fettucini and stir well to keep it from sticking. Boil the pasta until it is cooked through, 2 to 3 minutes for fresh, 8 to 10 minutes for dried.

Meanwhile, heat a medium skillet over medium-high heat and add the butter, spreading it so that it evenly coats the bottom of the pan. When the butter stops sizzling, add the shallots and mushrooms. Cook, stirring continuously, until the mushrooms soften, about 3 minutes. Add the cream and salmon and stir until the liquid reduces by half, about 2 minutes. Turn off the heat.

Drain the pasta in a colander and transfer it to a large pasta bowl. Use a rubber spatula to scrape the sauce over the pasta and toss gently so the noodles are lightly coated. Serve topped with a sprinling of parsley.

penne from the cupboard

SERVES 4

This is when the wisdom and foresight you showed stocking the pantry pays off. This dish practically makes itself. Open a bottle of Chianti to go with it and you won't believe that only twenty minutes ago, when you walked in the door after work, you had no inkling about what you were going to make for dinner. To speed the process up even more, the sauce can be made the day before and refrigerated. Leftover pasta can be easily reheated for lunch the following day.

12 ounces dried penne

2 tablespoons olive oil

$1/2$ medium onion, thinly sliced

1 (6-ounce) jar artichoke hearts, drained

1 (6-ounce) jar roasted red bell peppers, drained and cut into thin strips

1 (6-ounce) can tuna, drained and flaked

4 sun-dried tomatoes packed in oil, thinly sliced

3 cloves garlic, minced

1 (14-ounce) can whole tomatoes, drained

$1/2$ cup chicken broth

4 tablespoons chopped fresh basil, or 1 teaspoon dried

Salt and pepper to taste

Freshly grated Parmesan, for garnish

Fill an 8-quart pot two-thirds full of water and bring it to a boil over high heat. Add the penne and stir to keep it from sticking. Cook the pasta until it is al dente, 8 to 10 minutes.

Meanwhile, heat a large skillet over medium-high heat and add the oil, spreading it so that it evenly coats the bottom of the pan. Add the onion, artichoke hearts, roasted peppers, tuna, and sun-dried tomatoes. Cook, stirring continuously, until the onion softens, about 3 minutes. Add the garlic and cook 1 minute more. Add the tomatoes and break them up with a wooden spoon. Add the chicken broth and stir until the liquid reduces by half, about 3 minutes. Add the basil, salt, and pepper and stir to combine.

Drain the pasta in a colander and transfer it to a large pasta bowl. Pour the sauce over it and toss gently so the noodles are lightly coated. Sprinkle grated Parmesan generously over the top, and serve.

speedy tortellini

SERVES *2*

As if work wasn't enough to exhaust you, you valiantly decided to hit the gym on the way home. To get yourself over the last hill on the stationary bike, you imagine the plate of pasta waiting for you at home. But who's going to cook it? You are, once you experience the ease of this recipe. This fresh, light sauce is a gift from my friend Richard, who relies on it often after coming home from work. He minces the shallots and garlic and slices up the cherry tomatoes and shiitakes the night before, storing them in separate covered bowls or containers so they're ready to use.

12 ounces cheese tortellini

2 tablespoons olive oil

3 shallots, minced

$^1/_2$ pint cherry tomatoes, cut in half

4 ounces shiitake, cremini, or white mushrooms, thinly sliced

2 cloves garlic, minced

$^1/_2$ cup chicken broth

4 tablespoons chopped fresh basil, or 1 teaspoon dried

Salt and pepper to taste

Fill an 8-quart pot two-thirds full of water and bring it to a boil over high heat. Add the tortellini and stir well to keep it from sticking. Boil the pasta until it is cooked through, 2 to 3 minutes for fresh, 8 to 10 minutes for frozen or dried.

Meanwhile, heat a medium skillet over medium-high heat and add the oil, spreading it so that it evenly coats the bottom of the pan. Add the shallots, cherry tomatoes, and mushrooms. Cook, stirring continuously, until the mushrooms soften, about 3 minutes. Add the garlic and cook 1 minute more. Add the chicken broth and stir until the liquid reduces by half, about 2 minutes. Add the basil, salt, and pepper.

Drain the pasta in a colander and transfer it to a large pasta bowl. Use a rubber spatula to scrape the sauce over the pasta and toss gently so the noodles are lightly coated. Serve immediately.

baked penne

SERVES 6

Here's a quick and easy dish to serve when you're having a little dinner party. A quiet gathering with two other couples. Perhaps you're celebrating that you finally got your bed off the floor, or that you threw out those beer signs, or that you now have something inside your refrigerator besides condiments and peanut butter. Serve this pasta with steamed fresh vegetables and a salad and you've got yourself a swell dinner.

1 pound dried penne

1 (28-ounce) can crushed tomatoes

1 cup heavy whipping cream

10 ounces white mushrooms, thinly sliced

2 cups grated fontina (8 ounces)

2 teaspoons salt

Pepper to taste

1 cup ricotta

Preheat the oven to 450 degrees F. Lightly grease a 9-by-13-inch casserole with butter or vegetable oil cooking spray.

Fill an 8-quart pot two-thirds full of water and bring it to a boil over high heat. Add the penne and stir well to keep it from sticking. Boil the pasta until it is cooked through, 2 to 3 minutes for fresh, 8 to 10 minutes for dried.

Meanwhile, place the tomatoes, cream, mushrooms, fontina, salt, and pepper in a large bowl and stir to combine.

Drain the pasta in a colander, transfer it to the bowl with the tomato mixture, and toss gently. Using a rubber spatula, scrape the mixture into the casserole. Spoon the ricotta over the top (it doesn't need to

be an even layer). Bake on the center rack of
the oven for 15 minutes, until the sauce is
bubbling. Remove from the oven and let cool
a few minutes before serving.

thai vegetable noodles

SERVES *2*

Every cuisine has its own noodle dish. This one is vegetarian and features a refreshing Thai flavor. The dish is on the light side, making it a suitable choice for dinner after you've wolfed down a hefty burger for lunch. Slice the vegetables, except the onion, the night before or the morning you are cooking the noodles and store them, covered, in the refrigerator.

5 tablespoons freshly squeezed lime juice

2 tablespoons Thai fish sauce (see Note)

1¹/₂ teaspoons brown sugar

¹/₂ pound dried vermicelli noodles

3 tablespoons vegetable oil

1 medium onion, thinly sliced

¹/₄ pound shiitake mushrooms, stemmed and thinly sliced

2 medium celery stalks, thinly sliced

1 medium red bell pepper, cored, seeded, and thinly sliced

1 tablespoon minced fresh ginger, or 1 teaspoon ground ginger

3 tablespoons chopped fresh cilantro

In a small bowl, stir together the lime juice, fish sauce, and brown sugar until the sugar is dissolved. If using ground ginger, stir it into the sauce.

Fill an 8-quart pot two-thirds full of water and bring it to a boil over high heat. When the water boils, add the pasta and stir to keep it from sticking. Cook the pasta until it is al dente and drain in a colander. Transfer drained noodles to a medium bowl. Pour 1 tablespoon of the oil over the pasta and toss gently.

Heat a large skillet over high heat and add the remaining 2 tablespoons of oil, spreading it so that it evenly coats the bottom of the pan. Heat the oil just until it starts smoking. Add the onions, mushrooms, celery, red bell pepper, and fresh ginger and cook, stirring continuously, until the vegetables soften slightly, about 3 minutes. Add the cooked pasta to the pan and stir in the cilantro. Pour the sauce over the noodles and toss gently with a pasta fork or with tongs until the pasta is coated with the sauce. Serve immediately.

notes: Other vegetables, such as snow peas, sugar snap peas, broccoli or cauliflower florets, and green beans, can be substituted or added.

Thai fish sauce is widely available in most gourmet markets, health food stores, and Asian markets. It's the soy sauce of Thai cooking, though it is seldom used on its own the way soy sauce sometimes is used.

SOUPS, SALADS & SANDWICHES

WORKING STIFFS NEED to be resourceful when it comes to preparing their meals. Sometimes that means looking beyond the usual choices for dinner. That's where soups, salads, and sandwiches come in.

Soup and a sandwich make an admirable meal. The soup paces you, keeps you from surging through your food. It invites a slow fox-trot to the rhythm of the spoon.

Salads are quick, healthful, and easy to prepare. And now that many varieties of washed and cut lettuces are available in the produce section of most supermarkets, there's really no excuse for not making salads an integral part of your diet.

And don't overlook the fact that soups, salads, and sandwiches make a great lunch. As a Working Stiff, I have a love/hate relationship with lunch. I need it, I look forward to it, and I relish the time away from work. But lunchtime is also fraught with both culinary and existential dilemmas—where and what to eat, getting back to work on time, not staining my tie. If I buy my lunch instead of bringing it with me, I often spend much of my lunch hour waiting on line to get my food. It almost doesn't matter what I eat, as I hardly have the time to taste it. In reality, lunch on the fly isn't really lunch at all, it's just some grotesque parody of a meal.

Taking leftovers to work is one way a Working Stiff can get out of the lunch conundrum. You avoid having to decide what to eat, and you can lunch at a more leisurely pace since you're not using up your hour waiting on line to get your food. Soups, salads, and sandwiches are great ways to use up leftovers. Pieces of cooked chicken or meat are welcome additions to most soups and salads and they can be sliced for sandwiches.

On weekends, you may want to take the time to prepare a more indulgent lunch, one that you can savor before you drift off into a well-deserved nap.

grandma sally's easy broccoli soup

This recipe has been refined by Grandma Sally to where it's a cinch to make and results in a smooth and flavorful soup that doesn't use any cream.

1 medium head broccoli

1 medium tart apple (such as Rome, Granny Smith, or Golden Delicious), peeled, cored, and quartered

1 medium onion, sliced

6 cups chicken broth

1 teaspoon salt

1/4 teaspoon cayenne pepper

Low fat sour cream, for garnish

Cut the stem off the broccoli and separate the florets into large clusters. Trim a few inches off the bottom of the stem and cut the remaining portion into 1/2-inch pieces.

Place all of the ingredients into a 4-quart soup pot and bring to a boil over high heat. Reduce the heat to medium-low, cover, and simmer for 12 minutes.

Purée the soup in a blender or food processor in four batches, using equal parts solids and liquid to help make a smooth purée. Pour each batch of puréed soup into a large bowl or medium saucepan, if not serving immediately. Stir well, and adjust seasoning. To serve, ladle soup into bowls and garnish each bowl with a dollop of the sour cream.

sausage, escarole & white bean soup

SERVES 4

This soup and a loaf of crusty bread (baked by crusty bakers) makes a hearty meal. It would be great for a lunch on a cold winter's day after you've been out shoveling snow from the front walk (if you're lucky enough to have a front walk). You could easily make a double batch and freeze the extra to serve as a hearty first course for dinner.

1 tablespoon olive oil

$^1/_2$ pound smoked sausage (such as chorizo, kielbasa, or andouille), cut into $^1/_2$-inch-thick pieces

1 medium onion, chopped

4 cloves garlic, minced

1 large baking potato, cut into cubes

6 cups chicken broth

1 (15-ounce) can white beans, drained

1 medium head escarole, washed and cut into 1-inch pieces

Heat a 4-quart pot over medium-high heat and add the oil, spreading it so that it evenly coats the bottom of the pan. Add the sausage and onion and cook, stirring continuously, until the onions soften, about 3 minutes. Add the garlic and cook 1 minute more. Add the potato and broth and bring to a boil. Reduce the heat to medium-low, cover, and simmer for 18 minutes.

Add the beans and escarole and stir them into the soup. Cook for 5 minutes more. Serve immediately.

butternut squash soup

SERVES 4

The fact that this soup requires no sautéing and no stock will endear it to you. Instead of saying, "It's easy as apple pie," your new favorite adage will be "It's easy as butternut squash soup." This is a light, smooth soup that's versatile enough to serve at lunch with a salad or as the first course in an elegant dinner.

1 medium butternut squash

1 medium onion, chopped

2 cloves garlic

6 cups water

$1/4$ cup Port or dry sherry

$1/2$ teaspoon ground ginger

$1/2$ teaspoon ground coriander

$1/2$ teaspoon ground cinnamon

$1/4$ teaspoon ground cloves

1 teaspoon salt

Pepper to taste

Plain yogurt, for garnish

Chopped parsley, for garnish

To prepare the squash: Peel the squash with a vegetable peeler and trim each end. Cut the squash in half lengthwise and scoop out the seeds. Place the flat side on a cutting board and cut each half lengthwise. Cut the quarters crosswise to make 2-inch cubes.

Put all of the ingredients in a large pot and bring to a boil over a high heat. Stir briefly, reduce the heat to medium-low, and simmer for 18 minutes, until the squash is just cooked through.

Purée the soup in a blender or food processor in four batches, using equal parts solids and liquid to help make a smooth purée. Pour each batch of puréed soup into a large bowl or medium saucepan, if not serving immediately. Stir well, and adjust the seasoning. To serve, ladle soup into bowls and garnish each bowl with a dollop of the yogurt and a sprinkling of parsley.

portobello & onion sandwich

SERVES *2*

Meaty portobello mushrooms are showing up in lots of dishes, and for good reason. They have a flavor big enough to stand up to a sandwich. And, along with some potato salad, this is just the kind of sandwich you could easily serve for dinner.

3 tablespoons olive oil

1/2 medium onion, cut lengthwise into thin slices

2 medium portobello mushrooms, stemmed and cut into 1/2-inch-thick slices

1/2 teaspoon chopped fresh or dried rosemary

Salt and pepper to taste

4 thick slices Italian bread

2 tablespoons balsamic vinegar

Heat a large frying pan over medium-high heat and add the oil, spreading it so that it evenly coats the bottom of the pan. When the oil is hot, add the onions and mushrooms and cook, stirring frequently, until the onions soften, about 6 minutes. Add the rosemary and cook 1 minute more. Season with salt and pepper.

Divide the mushroom and onion mixture between 2 pieces of the bread and drizzle 1 tablespoon of balsamic vinegar over it. Top with the remaining piece of bread and serve immediately.

potato salad

SERVES 4

This is the consummate accompaniment to countless sandwiches. This version doesn't swamp the potatoes in mayonnaise, but if that's what you're used to, feel free to add more.

dressing

$^1/_2$ cup mayonnaise

1 tablespoon Dijon mustard

1 tablespoon white wine vinegar

1 pound Yukon Gold or red new potatoes

1 medium celery stalk, thinly sliced

1 kirby cucumber, cut into $^1/_2$-inch dice

2 scallions, cut into $^1/_2$-inch pieces

$^1/_4$ cup chopped fresh parsley

Salt and pepper to taste

To make the dressing: Mix together all of the ingredients in a mixing bowl and set aside.

Rinse the potatoes well and place them in a 2$^1/_2$-quart saucepan two-thirds full of cold water. Bring the water to a boil. Reduce the heat and simmer, uncovered, until the potatoes are tender yet firm, about 20 minutes. Drain the potatoes, transfer them to a cutting board, and cut them coarsely into quarters. Put the potatoes in a large mixing bowl and add the celery, cucumber, and scallions. Toss gently. Use a rubber spatula to scrape the dressing over the potato mixture. Sprinkle it with the parsley and gently toss until coated with the dressing. Serve immediately, or refrigerate, sealed well, up to 24 hours.

egg salad sandwich

SERVES 2

Had one of these lately? Because of concerns about cholesterol and fat, this sandwich has fallen out of favor. But there is something about egg salad on white bread that is unique—a quietness, a softness. This is definitely the sandwich to have on a Saturday afternoon after a week that really took it out of you.

4 large hard-boiled eggs, peeled (See Note)

1 medium celery stalk, diced

1/4 cup diced red onion

1/2 cup mayonnaise

Salt and pepper to taste

4 slices white bread

Lettuce and sliced tomato (optional)

Cut 1 egg in half lengthwise. Place each half flat side down on a cutting board and coarsely chop. Transfer the chopped egg to a medium bowl. Repeat with the remaining 3 eggs. Add the celery, onion, and mayonnaise to the bowl and stir. Season with salt and pepper.

Place half of the egg salad on a piece of bread. Top with lettuce and tomato, if desired. Add the top piece of bread, cut in half, and serve. Repeat for the remaining sandwich.

note: To make hard-boiled eggs, place the eggs gently in a 2½-quart saucepan two-thirds full of cold water. Do not drop them in or they may crack. Bring the water to a boil over medium-high heat. Reduce the heat to medium-low and simmer for 12 minutes. Remove the eggs with a slotted spoon and plunge them into a bowl of very cold water to stop the cooking process and make them easier to peel.

b.a.l.t.

This is the classic B.L.T. with the addition of some sliced avocado.

6 slices cooked bacon

4 slices white or wheat bread

1 medium avocado, sliced

2 large pieces romaine, Boston, or iceberg lettuce

1 medium tomato, sliced

2 tablespoons mayonnaise (optional)

Place 3 slices of bacon on a piece of bread. Top with half of the avocado slices, lettuce, and tomato. Spread 1 tablespoon of mayonnaise on a second piece of bread, if desired, and place the bread on top. Cut in half and serve.

note: An avocado is ready to eat when its color has darkened and when it is soft but not mushy. To open one, use a paring knife. Cut into the avocado lengthwise. When you come to the hard center pit, work the knife around, cutting through the meat as you go. Open the avocado and remove the pit with a spoon. Run the spoon between the meat and the skin and scoop out the meat in one piece. Place each half flat side down on a cutting board and slice. Avocados darken quickly, so prepare the avocado just before making the sandwich.

chicken & smoked mozzarella salad

SERVES *2*

This snazzy, colorful salad is a great way to use up leftover chicken and some of the vegetables that may be languishing in your fridge. It's a perfect summer lunch on the patio or light dinner you can enjoy when you're picnicking by the side of the road in the shade of your vintage Triumph Sportster. Leftover cooked green beans or broccoli can supplement or replace the vegetables in this recipe. Plain mozzarella or harder cheeses, such as Cheddar or Swiss, can replace the smoked mozzarella.

4 tablespoons extra-virgin olive oil

2 tablespoons balsamic vinegar

1 clove garlic, minced

1 teaspoon chopped fresh or dried rosemary

2 cups cooked chicken, cut into 1-inch dice

1 medium yellow bell pepper, cored, seeded, and cut into 1-inch dice

2 medium celery stalks, cut into $^1/_2$-inch pieces

12 cherry tomatoes, cut in half

$^1/_2$ pound smoked mozzarella, cut into $^1/_2$-inch cubes

4 tablespoons chopped fresh basil, or 1 teaspoon dried

Several leaves romaine or Boston lettuce, washed and dried

Place the oil, vinegar, garlic, and rosemary in a large mixing bowl and stir until well combined. Add the chicken and toss so it is well coated. Add the remaining ingredients, except the lettuce, and toss well. Serve on a bed of the lettuce leaves.

grilled cheese sandwich

SERVES **2**

You can make a simple grilled cheese sandwich, or you can make a daring grilled cheese sandwich. Use individually wrapped slices of American cheese or a richly flavored English farm Cheddar or French Gruyère. Any way you do it, a grilled cheese sandwich will always be sublime.

3 to 4 ounces American, Cheddar, Swiss, Gruyère, Cottswald, or other hard or semi-soft cheese, thinly sliced

4 slices bread

2 tablespoons butter

Divide the cheese between two slices of bread, covering evenly. Lightly butter the remaining two slices of bread with 1 tablespoon of the butter and place on top of the cheese, butter side up.

Place a large skillet on medium heat. Add the butter, spreading it so that it evenly coats the bottom of the pan. When the butter stops sizzling, place the sandwiches in the pan, buttered side up. Cook until the bottoms are nicely brown, about 4 minutes. Turn and cook 4 minutes more. Serve immediately.

variations: Thinly sliced ham, smoked turkey, tomato, pepperoncini, or onion can be added in any combination to the sandwich before grilling. Just beware of making the sandwich too thick, as it will keep the cheese from melting thoroughly.

citrus shrimp salad

SERVES 2

A tangy, refreshing tropical salad that's great on a hot summer day. Try this at poolside with a tall, blended fruit drink.

dressing

$^1/_3$ cup freshly squeezed orange juice

3 tablespoons freshly squeezed lime juice

2 tablespoons extra-virgin olive oil

2 teaspoons honey

1 teaspoon balsamic vinegar

$^1/_2$ teaspoon Dijon mustard

Salt and pepper to taste

12 ounces medium shrimp, cleaned and deveined

$^1/_2$ medium fennel bulb, peeled and diced (see Note page 99)

$^1/_2$ medium red bell pepper, cored, seeded, and diced

$^1/_2$ medium red onion, diced

1 medium celery stalk, diced

2 scallions, finely chopped

1 tablespoon chopped fresh coriander, or $^1/_2$ teaspoon dried

Several leaves romaine or Boston lettuce, washed and dried

to make the dressing:

Mix together all of the ingredients in a medium bowl and set aside.

Fill a 2$^{1}/_{2}$-quart saucepan two-thirds full of water and bring it to a bowl over high heat. Add the shrimp and cook until they turn pink and are just cooked through, about 3 minutes. Drain the shrimp in a colander and refresh under cold water. Transfer the shrimp to a large bowl.

Add the remaining ingredients, except the lettuce, to the bowl with the shrimp and toss gently. Pour the dressing over and toss so that all of the shrimp are completely coated. Refrigerate for 1 hour. Serve on individual plates, spooned onto the lettuce leaves.

frozen banana
strawberry shake

SERVES 2

This is just the drink to cool you down when the temperature starts going up.

*1 cup hulled fresh or
    frozen strawberries*
1 ripe banana
$^{1}/_{2}$ cup vanilla yogurt
$^{1}/_{2}$ cup orange juice
*1 tablespoon freshly
    squeezed lime juice*
1$^{1}/_{2}$ cups crushed ice

Put all of the ingredients in a blender and purée until smooth. Pour into tall glasses and serve immediately.

leftover lo mein

Lo mein may not have been meant for leftovers, but throw any leftover chicken, beef, pork, shellfish, or vegetables into the pasta and you'll have a quick and fabulous lunch. Unless they've got a camp stove and a wok outside your front door, you can make this faster than the local Chinese restaurant can deliver it. Needless to say, it'll taste better, too.

sauce

¹/₂ cup soy sauce

¹/₄ cup dry white wine

1 tablespoon brown sugar

1 teaspoon curry powder

1 teaspoon ground ginger

12 ounces thin vermicelli noodles

1 tablespoon vegetable oil

1 cup leftover beef, chicken, pork, or shellfish, cut into thin slivers

1 medium onion, thinly sliced

2 carrots, grated

4 ounces snow peas, top strings removed (see Note)

4 ounces mung bean sprouts

Place the ingredients for the sauce into a small bowl and stir together until well combined. Set aside.

Fill a large pot with water and bring it to boil over high heat. Add the noodles to the boiling water and stir to keep them from sticking. Cook until the noodles are al dente and drain in a colander.

While the water is boiling, heat a large skillet over high heat and add the oil, spreading it so that it evenly coats the bottom of the pan. When the oil is hot, add the onions and cook, stirring frequently, until they soften, about 3 minutes. Add the garlic and cook 1 minute more. Add the remaining ingredients and cook until everything is heated through. Finally, add the drained pasta and the sauce and stir everything together.

note: If you have kids, as a novelty, try adding a few ears of canned baby corn along with the other vegetables.

leftover wild rice salad

SERVES 4

This makes a great summer lunch. You may even want to take it on a picnic, even if you're just sitting on a park bench during a lunch break. You can close your eyes and pretend you're in the French country-side, lounging in the afternoon sun with a bottle of wine and a volume of Baudelaire. But, if you're going to indulge in this reverie, make sure you aren't sitting under a tree filled with pigeons.

4 cups cooked wild rice

2 carrots, grated

1 medium yellow pepper, diced

2 medium celery stalks, diced

2 scallions, chopped

1 cup green seedless grapes, cut in half

$^1/_4$ cup orange juice

2 tablespoons red wine vinegar

1 teaspoon Dijon mustard

1 teaspoon salt

$^1/_4$ cup extra virgin olive oil

Put the rice, carrots, yellow pepper, celery, scallions, and grapes in a medium mixing bowl. In a small mixing bowl, whisk together the orange juice, vinegar, mustard, and salt. Drizzle in the olive oil as you continue whisking. Pour the dressing over the salad and toss until the rice is coated.

Serve immediately or refrigerate in a well-sealed container for up to 6 hours.

note: If you want to prepare this more than 6 hours ahead of time, store the rice mixture and dressing separately and toss them together just before serving.

leftover green bean salad

SERVES 4

If you cook an extra pound of green beans you'll have enough left over to make this colorful salad. It also works well with leftover broccoli florets.

1 pound cooked green beans

1 medium yellow bell pepper, thinly sliced

12 cherry tomatoes, cut in half

4 tablespoons chopped fresh basil or 1 teaspoon dried

3 tablespoons red wine vinegar

1/2 teaspoon Dijon mustard

Salt and pepper to taste

4 tablespoons extra virgin olive oil

Put the green beans, yellow pepper, cherry tomatoes, and basil in a salad bowl. In a small bowl whisk together the vinegar, mustard, salt and pepper. Drizzle in the olive oil as you continue whisking. Pour the dressing over the vegetables and toss gently. Season with salt and pepper to taste, if needed.

note: 1 cup of chopped, cooked chicken or thinly sliced ham, prosciutto, or Italian salami could be added to this salad for some extra substance.

eggs for dinner

SERVES **4**

There's nothing faster to cook than eggs. You can beat them while the pan is heating up, and cook them while the toast is toasting. The Scrambler is like an omelet, only not quite as urbane. Here, zesty fillings like grated cheese, diced ham, bell peppers, and scallions are added. Eggs-in-the-Hole might bring you back to a rustic cabin in Maine when your dad cooked them up in a black, cast iron skillet. Serve with broiled tomatoes and some fresh fruit for a fast, light dinner.

the scrambler

5 large eggs

$^1/_2$ cup (1 ounce) grated cheese, such as Cheddar, Gruyère, or Fontina

$^1/_4$ cup diced ham or cooked bacon

$^1/_2$ medium red bell pepper, cored seeded, and diced

1 scallion, chopped

1 tablespoon butter

Beat the eggs in a medium mixing bowl. Add the cheese, ham, bell pepper, and scallions and stir to combine.

Place a large skillet on high heat. Add the butter and spread it so it coats the bottom of the pan. When the butter stops sizzling, add the egg mixture and cook, stirring continuously, until the eggs are set. Serve immediately.

variations: Add sliced sautéed mushrooms, zucchini, or other vegetables to the beaten eggs before cooking. For a more sublime Scrambler, substitute $^1/_4$ pound chopped, smoked salmon for the diced ham.

eggs-in-the-hole

4 slices bread

1 tablespoon butter

4 eggs

With a cookie cutter or a knife, cut a 2-inch wide hole in the center of each slice of bread.

Place a large skillet on medium-high heat. Add the butter, spreading it so that it evenly coats the bottom of the pan. When the butter stops sizzling, add the bread slices, and immediately, but carefully, crack one of the eggs over the hole in one of the bread slices, making sure the yolk slips into the hole. Repeat with the remaining 3 eggs and bread slices. Cook until the whites almost set, about 1 minute. With a metal spatula, gently turn over each slice of bread. Cook about 30 seconds more, until all the white is fully set (the yellow should still be a bit loose). Serve immediately.

broiled tomatoes

SERVES 2

A standard part of the classic English breakfast which makes a great addition to any dinner.

4 tablespoons unseasoned bread crumbs

1 tablespoon freshly grated Parmesan

$1/2$ teaspoon salt

2 medium ripe tomatoes, cut in half

Pepper to taste

Preheat the broiler.

In a shallow bowl, mix together the bread crumbs, Parmesan cheese, and salt until well combined. Lay the cut side of one tomato in the bread crumb mixture, then place it on a broiler-proof pan, crumb side up. Repeat with remaining tomato halves.

Broil the tomatoes 6 inches from the heat until the tops are brown and crusty, about 4 minutes. Season with pepper to taste. Serve immediately.

greek salad in pita sandwich

SERVES 2

You can serve Greek salad on a plate, but I much prefer it in a pita. It's a lot more manageable this way and makes a great summer lunch on the patio or by the pool. This recipe makes four sandwiches, which, in my mind, is just right to serve two. Serve with some refreshing melon and liqueur for a fun and easy summer lunch or light dinner.

$^1/_2$ medium head romaine or Boston lettuce, cut into 1-inch pieces

2 ounces feta cheese, crumbled

6 cherry tomatoes, cut in half

12 pitted Kalamata or other black olives

$^1/_2$ medium red onion, thinly sliced

$^1/_2$ medium cucumber, cut lengthwise then thinly sliced

1 (6-ounce) jar artichoke hearts, drained and coarsely chopped

6 tablespoons vinaigrette

2 pitas

Place all the ingredients except the vinaigrette and pita in a large bowl. Add the vinaigrette and toss gently. Cut the pitas in half, open them, and fill each pocket with salad. Do not overstuff. Serve immediately.

note: If you want to pack these sandwiches for a trip or picnic, do not dress the salad before stuffing the pitas as the dressing will make the bread soggy. Pack the dressing separately and drizzle it on just before serving.

melon surprise

SERVES **2**

This is a very refreshing
dessert for a hot summer night.

> *¹/₂ tablespoon kirsch, anisette or*
> *other liqueur*
> *1 tablespoon confectioners' sugar*
> *2 tablespoons water*
> *1 ripe cantaloupe, halved and seeded*

In a small bowl, combine the kirsch,
sugar, and water.

With a melon baller, scoop out the
melon flesh into little balls and place them in
a serving bowl. Pour the kirsch mixture over
the melon balls and toss gently until all of the
fruit is covered with syrup. Place in the refrigerator for at least 1 hour and up to 3 hours to
macerate before serving.

note: Hulled strawberries and/or
raspberries can be added to replace the melon.

NOTES

INDEX

TABLE OF EQUIVALENTS

The exact equivalents in the following tables have been rounded for convenience.

Liquid and Dry Measures

U.S.	Metric
¹/₄ teaspoon	1.25 milliliters
¹/₂ teaspoon	2.5 milliliters
1 teaspoon	5 milliliters
1 tablespoon (3 teaspoons)	15 milliliters
1 fluid ounce (2 tablespoons)	30 milliliters
¹/₄ cup	60 milliliters
¹/₃ cup	80 milliliters
1 cup	240 milliliters
1 pint (2 cups)	480 milliliters
1 quart (4 cups, 32 ounces)	960 milliliters
1 gallon (4 quarts)	3.84 liters
1 ounce (by weight)	28 grams
1 pound	454 grams
2.2 pounds	1 kilogram

Length Measures

U.S.	Metric
¹/₈ inch	3 millimeters
¹/₄ inch	6 millimeters
¹/₂ inch	12 millimeters
1 inch	2.5 centimeters

Oven Temperatures

Fahrenheit	Celsius	Gas
250	120	¹/₂
275	140	1
300	150	2
325	160	3
350	180	4
375	190	5
400	200	6
425	220	7
450	230	8
475	240	9
500	260	10